MW00534015

Temple Stay

A Journey of Self-Discovery

KOREA ESSENTIALS No. 17

Temple Stay: A Journey of Self-Discovery

Copyright © 2014 by The Korea Foundation

Published in 2014 by Seoul Selection
B1 Korean Publishers Association Bldg., 6 Samcheng-ro, Jongno-gu, Seoul
110-190, Korea
Phone: (82-2) 734-9567
Fax: (82-2) 734-9562
Email: publisher@seoulselection.com
Website: www.seoulselection.com

ISBN: 978-89-97639-49-6   04080
ISBN: 978-89-91913-70-7   (set)
Printed in the Republic of Korea

Temple Stay

A Journey of Self-Discovery

KOREA FOUNDATION
한국국제교류재단

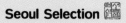

Seoul Selection

CONTENTS

Appendix
Information 108

Delving Deeper

INTRODUCTION

Travel has been described by many as a person's greatest teacher because the experience of making different connections in a new place offers wisdom that can be used to deal with other aspects of one's life. Benefiting from it, however, requires an open mind for learning. What is the concept of a temple stay that this book seeks to introduce? Can one night spent at a temple, the repository of Korea's Buddhist culture and spirit, be our teacher? The answer from those who have experienced it is "Yes."

A temple stay is a short sojourn at a temple where one follows monastic rules of life. For this reason, many seek out temples for the explicit purpose of having a rest. It is for this reason that a temple stay can be compared to a nap: a short break from one's daily routines provides the energy necessary for carrying on with one's busy existence. But before you view temple stays as

simply a type of short vacation, keep in mind that the temple stay experience is about so much more than rest.

The various temple stay programs offered around the country all possess, to some degree, the essence of Korean Buddhism. This book uses simple terms to explain the meaning of some of the rituals that one may encounter at a temple stay, such as performing 108 prostrations while threading 108 prayer beads, conversing with monks over tea, or making lanterns in the shape of a lotus, a symbol of Buddhism. It also intends to explain the meaning behind *barugongyang*, a dining method carried out since the time of the historical Buddha Shakyamuni. Through this practice, one becomes aware of the efforts put forth on behalf of all beings in the making of food, not least of all being nature, which consists of earth, wind, the sun, and water.

The book also introduces special temple stay programs, as it is helpful to learn about the sort of experiences offered by temple stays besides rest, and apply to partake in them. From the Buddhist martial art known as *sunmudo* or the roasting of coffee beans to walking through a 1,000-year-old forest of fir trees, enjoying the blue waves of the East Sea, or learning to be one with a waterfall, there are many different kinds of programs that are outlined in this publication. In addition to describing Korean Buddhist practices that are possible to experience through temple stays, this volume also includes explanations for practices that can be carried out in everyday life, shared with the hope that some of the insights obtained through temple stays can also be obtained outside the temple setting.

The Korean Buddhist temples that host temple stays are always very sacred and historic places. As a courtesy, it is helpful to understand some of the basic means of showing respect to Buddhist spaces so as to avoid committing offenses simply out of ignorance about temples. The depth of your experience can be more profound if you participate in a temple stay with an understanding of what temple structures signify. As stated in the popular adage, knowledge is power, and knowing more about something will improve your overall experience.

For example, there is no reason to fear the four terrifying statues situated at the entrance to most temples. In this book, we explain the meaning of these figures—posed at what is known as the Gate of the Four Heavenly Kings—as well as the much less ominous One Pillar Gate on the very edge of a temple, and everything in between: the dharma hall, stone lanterns, and other structures inside the temple precinct. Also included in this book are instructions for basic temple etiquette, such as what to do when entering the dharma hall, when exploring the temples or temple grounds, and when meeting a monk. Along similar lines, the book addresses some of the reasons

why it is important to avoid wearing revealing clothing, as well as brief introduction for how a day at the temple progresses—all intended to help make your temple stay experience a positive one.

The subtleties and symbolism tucked away in the different corners of a temple can be appreciated on a much deeper level if one is familiar with the 1,700-year history of Korean Buddhism. Here, we organize the history of Korean Buddhism from its transmission to its renaissance. We also try to enhance your understanding of Korean Buddhism by adding an explanation of *ganhwaseon* meditation practiced in Korean Buddhism, commonly known as Seon Buddhism.

Finally, we have included a list of home pages and contact information for temples that are worth seeking out because of their noteworthy temple stay programs.

Are you ready to transcend the boundary of religion and depart for a temple stay, the storehouse of Korean Buddhist culture? Open your mind to the information contained in this book.

"Do not go to the garden of flowers!
O friend! Go not there;
In your body is the garden of flowers."

– The Indian poet and ascetic Kabir

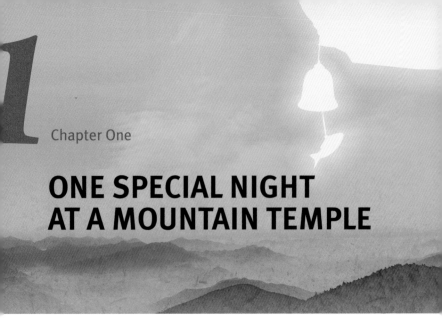

ONE SPECIAL NIGHT AT A MOUNTAIN TEMPLE

I got up at three in the morning. Drawn to the sound of the temple drum and bell, I attended the morning service, bowed 108 times, ate a four-bowl meal without leaving a single grain of rice or red pepper flake, meditated, and walked barefoot in the mountains. My two days and one night spent at a Buddhist temple were truly memorable, to say the least.

"When you participate in a temple stay," said one of the monks I spoke with, "abandon the desire to gain something for yourself. The more you abandon before you come, the more you can gain."

The temple stay program began with putting one's personal items—cell phone and wallet, typically, though cigarettes as well, if applicable—in a basket. There was one final minute for a quick phone call before the cell phones were left behind; the participants use that time to say brief goodbyes to their families and loved ones, or tend to unfinished business. Then we changed into monk's robes and sat awkwardly as the monk in charge of the program explained the basic rules of temple life. The two most important things seemed to be "folding hands" (*chasu*) and the "procession of geese" (*anhaeng*).

"We fold our hands by placing them one above the other just over the lower abdomen. When you move around the temple, you should maintain this position," said the leader. "When you walk, please walk in single file like geese. We call this a 'procession of geese.' We must always maintain a cautious attitude and state of mind, as if walking on thin ice."

Walking on thin ice? When I thought about it, this approach could describe my whole life up until that point. Hadn't my existence been one of simply running hastily on what I pretended was a broad, flat road, forgetting or ignoring the unfathomable drop one step to either side?

FULL-BODY BOWING

Because participants come from around the nation, most temple stay programs begin in the afternoon. The schedule was relatively light: We had tea with the monks and got used to our awkward robes, then worked up a proper appetite before the evening meal with a fragrant walk among the centuries-old pine trees of Mt. Taehwasan.

After a buffet-style evening meal, we learned the *jeol*, or full-body bow, a sort of rehearsal for the morning chanting service. The bow is performed by first bringing both knees to the ground, then bringing both arms together and bowing as low as possible so that your forehead touches the ground. We had seen it often enough on TV, but most of us were actually doing it for the first time ourselves. It is a common misconception that a full-body bow is only done with the limbs stretched out in the shape of a cross, as in Tibetan Buddhism. In a way, the Catholic priests' prostration before the cross during ordination is not so different from the Buddhist full-body bow.

When the monk made a play on words in Korean, saying, "We call it a *jeol* [temple] because we practice *jeol* [bowing] so much." he wasn't kidding. The mats spread out on the floor were visibly worn from the contact of countless knees and elbows. Bowing is an act of lowering oneself ultimately; it is a process of finding your true self hidden beneath all boasting and pretension, all anxiety and fear.

At a temple, even sleeping is a form of practice: meditation while lying down. You lie quietly with your hands on your lower belly, feeling the breath go in and out of your body. In this way, you look into your mind to see what thoughts go in and out. The monk told us we did not need to try to drive off the countless anxieties of the world that might flood in as we lay in the dark of this quiet mountain temple, but to simply look at them.

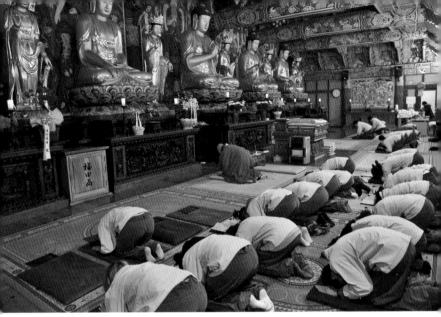

Full-body bowing (Geumsansa Temple, Jeollabuk-do)

Silence is observed from the moment you lie down until the moment you finish the morning meal the next day. You cannot even signal to or glance at others. The purpose of this practice is so that you can properly look into your own mind. Somewhere, someone is snoring lightly.

MORNING SERVICE

Three minutes past three in the morning. I woke to the sound of the wooden fish being struck to drive away the early dawn darkness. Everyone got up, folded their bedding, and gathered in front of the temple bell. Neither conversation nor glances were exchanged between anyone. The monk struck the cloud gong before moving to the front of the temple drum. Then, he struck the massive

Morning service (Haeinsa Temple, Gyeongsangnam-do)

instrument, much larger than himself, to wake up all living creatures that might still be asleep in the darkness. The sound of the drum cleaved the early morning air and echoed off Mt. Taehwasan, which enveloped the temple. The moon still shone brightly above the firs beyond Paradise Bridge.

As we listened to the bell being rung (33 times in total), we walked in single file, like geese, toward the main hall. After the short service, we bowed 108 times to the sharp clack of a bamboo clapper that a monk rapped in the palm of his hand. The monk told us to continue looking into our minds even as we bowed, but as my breathing grew heavier and my knees began to ache, I couldn't think of anything much. We finished the bowing earlier than I thought and knelt on the floor, but I was still uncomfortable and had a hard time gathering my thoughts.

After the morning service I arose on shaky legs and walked to the spring in front of the temple—still in silence, of course. As I walked across the stepping stones in the stream and along the path lined thick with reeds, I heard the sound of all life in heaven and on Earth awakening. My mind and body seemed to react to even the slightest stimulus, so much more so than in the city.

A TOUR OF THE TEMPLE

Soon it grew bright and the mountain temple was filled with birdsong. An odd "rat-tat-tat-tat" sound could be heard in the distance. Was it a drill digging into the earth at some distant construction site? I soon learned the origin of the sound—it was a woodpecker, which I had only seen in cartoons as a child. I looked around carefully, but I was never able to see it pecking away at a tree; I only saw its wings flapping as it flew away.

Touring the temple (Magoksa Temple, Chungcheongnam-do)

After the morning meal, when we were finally allowed to open our mouths again, the monk led us on a tour of the 1,000-year-old temple. Magoksa Temple sits in a beautiful valley with its grounds bisected by the gentle, winding waters of Taehwacheon Stream. On one side is a collection of simple buildings for monastic practice, with the more imposing structures for prayer situated on the other side. This is what sets Magoksa Temple apart from other temples: once past the ticket booth, although the temple is only a short walk away, you must trek quite a distance up the winding valley before actually reaching Enlightenment Gate, the main entrance, and the Gate of the Four Heavenly Kings beyond that.

We passed a small group of stupas, or shrines, and then looked around Vulture Peak Hall before passing through the Gate of the

Paradise Bridge in Magoksa Temple

Four Heavenly Kings, crossing over Paradise Bridge and arriving at the Precious Hall of Great Light, where the Vairocana Buddha is located. Beyond that is the Hall of the Great Hero dedicated to the Shakyamuni Buddha, where services are held to worship the Buddha three times a day. Temple stay participants are housed in a building next to the Precious Hall of Great Light. With its national treasures and numerous other cultural assets, this temple is an enchanted land in a mountain valley, its halls and pagodas sitting amid lush pine and cherry forests.

MEAL OF FOUR BOWLS

In temple life, lunch is known as the meal of four bowls (*barugongyang*). At a temple, even eating is a form of practice. We place our hands together at the sound of the bamboo clapper, and then arrange the four bowls in front of us according to size. The smallest bowl is first filled with water for washing out all your dishes at the end of the meal, and then the remaining bowls are filled with rice, soup, kimchi, and a few side dishes—however much you intend to eat.

Prior to eating, we take a piece of kimchi, rinse it thoroughly in the soup, and put it in the rice bowl. We then eat with as little sound or chopstick clatter as possible—without speaking, of course—and, when finished, we pour water into the rice bowl and wipe the rice, soup, and side dish bowls clean with the rinsed kimchi. Then we eat this piece of kimchi and drink the water. But this is not the end. The final step is to wash the bowls clean with the water from the smallest bowl; two-thirds of the water is thrown away, and the rest, filled with seasonings and grains of rice, you drink.

ON RETURNING TO EVERYDAY LIFE

Temple stay programs will differ somewhat depending on the participants, but I found that the most memorable activities were when we "looked into our minds" on the first day and the barefoot walk through the mountains on the second day. Looking into one's mind involved having participants briefly introduce themselves before speaking honestly and candidly about their most difficult experiences or most earnest desires. Though perhaps very simple in theory, the act of calmly sharing your innermost thoughts with a group of strangers truly caused each of us to take a closer look at our own consciousness.

The barefoot walk around Mt. Taehwasan was an activity where participants meditated while walking barefoot for just over two hours. Despite the sense of solitude afforded by such a quiet hike, it was not a solemn walk from start to finish; after meditating during prescribed sections of the path, we talked about things that we had not yet shared, chatting and laughing like children on a picnic as we walked along leisurely. There were both flat sections and rough, rocky areas, but we did not mind; it was a time for us to control our thoughts and breathing, and to become one with nature.

After passing through the final gate as I was leaving the temple the next day, I thought of something I had been told by the program assistant when I signed up for the program:

Buddhism is characterized by a lack of limitations. We also

call this "the void." We accept everyone, with no preconditions. When you participate in the temple stay, abandon the desire to gain something for yourself. The more you abandon before you come, the more you can gain.

I don't know how many nights I will need to spend under the roof of a temple to sweep away all the dust that has built up, layer upon layer, in my mind over the 30-something years of my life, but I have at least decided to try it again in the near future.

2

TEMPLES:
THE SPACE OF PRACTICE

TEMPLES AS A WORLD OF SYMBOLS

Korean Buddhist temples can be largely divided into three categories: flat land, mountainside, and cave. The most common type among them, mountainside, refers to temples that are literally located on mountains, corresponding to the most representative image of Korean Buddhist temples. Such temples exist in striking harmony with the surrounding natural environment. Those that boast long histories and many traditions are especially good examples of how architecture can maximize the utility of a location while still allowing it to exist in harmony with nature.

But beyond architectural distinctions, the symbolism present in details common to all temples is also noteworthy.

A temple is designed to be an embodiment of the world of the Buddha, standing apart from the world of ordinary beings while still being accessible to everyone. From the gates of the temple's entry points to the highest spires of its pagodas, a temple complex is rich in symbolism, representing each and every step of the way to the Buddha. Although improvements in transit routes have now made it quite easy to visit temples, when ancient temples were first built, meeting the Buddha required a very difficult journey. Because of how demanding such journeys were known to be, the apparition of the Buddha, visible at last, must have seemed like ecstasy itself.

The Gate: Entering the World of the Buddha

The Buddha Pure Land denotes the place where the Buddha lives, as well as the temple that enshrines his image. Temples are a space meant to assist in achieving nirvana by providing access to the

Naksansado, Kim Hong-do, Joseon Dynasty, 1778. This painting shows a typical mountainside temple, corresponding to the most representative image of Korean Buddhist temples.

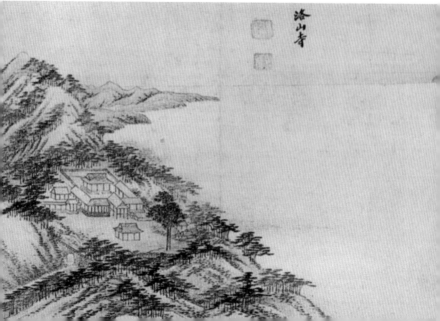

Buddha, and for this reason, they are open at all times so that people may come and meet the Buddha and encounter his teachings without restriction. The entryway to this world is marked by Iljumun—the One Pillar Gate. It is the first in a series of three gates that mark the entrance to a temple. The reference to "one" in its title reflects the fact that the middle of the gate is supported by a single row of pillars, not one lone pillar as the name may suggest.

The second gate is Cheonwangmun—the Gate of the Heavenly Kings—which enshrines the four kings who guard the four cardinal directions in Buddhist cosmology: Virudhaka, Dhrtarastra, Vaisravana, and Virupaksa. They protect the teaching of the Buddha and subdue evil beings, serving as guardians of the temple. The third and final gate is Bulimun—the Gate of Non-Duality. Sometimes called Haetalmun, or the Gate of Awakening, it stands just in front

Iljumun in a mountain (Gangcheonsa Temple, Jeollabuk-do)

of buildings that make up the center of the temple. The concept of non-duality mentioned in its name refers to truth—the idea that there is no difference between life and death, being and non-being. Non-duality, by contrast, is the state of absolute equality. The term embodies the Buddhist truth that all things are equal. Once you enter through to this world, you find yourself in a radically different existence.

Though the typical layout of Korean temples has changed over time, each space is normally designed to reflect the shape of Mt. Sumeru, a mythical peak that stands at the center of Buddhist cosmology. This mountain, which is believed to rise out of a great ocean, has three layers: At the bottom is the world of desire, which then briefly transitions into the celestial world. This is followed by the

Jeungjang-cheonwang (Virudhaka) is one of four guardian kings. He grips a dragon in his right hand and a *cintamani* (wish-granting jewel) in his left.

world of form, which consists of 18 heavens or worlds. The final layer is the formless world, which is composed of four heavens and is situated at the very top. The three layers of Mt. Sumeru—bottom, middle, and top—are mirrored in the layout of the temple. Between the One Pillar Gate at the entrance to the grounds—the bottom of the temple—and the Gate of Non-Duality at the top of the footpath leading in, there lies the celestial world where four musical instruments (*samul*) play the sound of propagation that leads every being between hell and the Buddhist paradise, moving forward on the path to becoming a Buddha him- or herself.

The One Pillar Gate corresponds with the bottom of the mountain, a transition from the realm of desire to the celestial world guarded by the Heavenly Kings. On passing through the Gate of Heavenly Kings, one soon enters the world of truth marked by the Gate of Non-Duality. This corresponds to the middle layer of Mt. Sumeru. Beyond the gate, there are various Buddhas who have understood the principle of all things. They reside at the top of the mountain, a space where lanterns, pagodas, and other grand buildings that make up the center of the temple can be found.

The Dharma Hall: Meeting the Buddha Who Watches over All Beings

The largest structure at the heart of the temple is the *beopdang*—the dharma hall—which may have a different name depending on the identity of the awakened one who resides within it. Looking at the panel hanging above the sliding doors in front can tell us the identity of the Buddha inside. If the sign says Daeungjeon or Daeungbojeon,

The three Buddha statues in the Daeungjeon

Baekyangsa Temple, Jeollanam-do

it is the Buddha Shakyamuni, the historic Buddha who was born some 26 centuries ago. If the placard says Geungnakjeon, it is the Buddha Amitabha, the Lord of the Western Paradise. Yaksajeon represents the Eastern Crystal Light Pure Land of the Medicine Buddha. The final possibility is Mireukjeon, which corresponds to the Tusita Heaven of the Buddha Maitreya who will appear one day to lead beings of this world toward salvation, and is therefore especially ornate.

While monks may pursue a life of detachment and content themselves with simple things and basic necessities, the dharma hall is a different story. Such majestic, resplendent spaces would be considered impressive to visitors from anywhere in the world. This is because the dharma hall represents the world of the Buddha, a place characterized by happiness, freedom, and absence of worry. Placed in the center of the room, the Buddha sits on an altar and looks down upon beings who gather before him, flanked by murals on the

Daeungbojeon, or dharma hall (Gakwonsa Temple, Chungcheongnam-do)

walls to the left and right. There are countless manifestations of him on the upper wall, emanating from his intense concentration. These manifestations are thought to be bodhisattvas—powerful Buddhist figures—who exist to save all beings. Auspicious symbols such as flying dragons, birds of paradise, and beautiful lotuses form a splendid pattern across the ceiling and the various pillars that support it. Every surface is decorated to the maximum, except for the wide space just in front of the Buddha; this area is reserved for those who come to see and hear him. By sitting in front of the Buddha in a hall that replicates the moment of the Buddha's most important sermon, we become part of the historical reenactment of the scene where the Buddha expounded his teaching before a great assembly.

Surrounding Daeungjeon are other halls such as Gwaneumjeon, Myeongbujeon, Jijangjeon, and Nahanjeon, which are each occupied by other awakened beings. This is the world of the Buddha and bodhisattvas, perfectly recreated in the form of temples and situated deep in the mountains of Korea.

Stone Lanterns: Lighting the Radiant Mind

Besides the various aforementioned halls, the legendary top of Mt. Sumeru also features stone lanterns and pagodas. While much smaller than the halls, they still have their own unique significance within Buddhist culture. As their name suggests, lanterns are meant for holding small lamps, their light not only symbolizing the awakening of the Buddha but also the light of truth and the light of the mind. They also serve to illuminate the darkness in one's mind— epitomized by ignorance—so that the mind itself will cast this cloud aside and become its own source of light, guiding each person in the search for the treasure that is the Buddha and the path toward Buddhahood.

Pagodas: Accumulation of Truth

If a lantern illuminates the path toward truth, a pagoda is truth itself. Pagodas originate from the practice of stupa worship in India where the historical Buddha passed away, leaving his body to be cremated, with resulting relics (bone fragments and special objects that only an eminent figure would produce) enshrined inside a mound. Such relics were treated as though they were the Buddha himself, and the mound, called stupa, became an object of pilgrimage and worship. Over time, stupa worship was transmitted from India to Korea via China, and in East Asia the mound form was replaced by that of a tower, which is known as *tap* in Korean but

Three-story stone pagoda with four-lion pedestal from the unified Silla period at Hwaeomsa Temple in Gurye, Jeollanam-do, National Treasure No.35

SAMUL: MUSICAL INSTRUMENTS FOR CONVERSION OF THE MASSES

In the early morning, or in the evening when the sky becomes crimson, four musical instruments unique to Korean temples make an appearance. Used in most ceremonies, their names are *beomjong*, *beopgo*, *mogeo*, and *unpan*. The aural imagery that first comes to mind when talking about Korean temples is the sound of *beomjong*; it gives off the best-known and most familiar sound.

A *beomjong* is a large bell used at temples. Its first syllable—*beom*—means "purity." The instrument represents the belief that those who hear the teaching of the Buddha at the same time they hear the sound of the bell can break the cycle of suffering involving death and life and attain awakening. The bell is rung in the hope that even those in hell will hear its sound, wrestle free from their place of existence, and enter the path of awakening. Its clear and majestic sound reverberates far and wide, bringing peace to anyone who hears it. The *beomjong* is also used as a signal to gather an assembly, and for this reason it also has the function of announcing the start of morning and evening worship.

Beomjong

If *beomjong* has a powerful aural impact, *beopgo*—a large drum clad in leather—appeals to both sight and sound. Traditionally, the performer will start off slowly before becoming increasingly faster over time, and the performer's movement will replicate the Chinese character for the mind—心, pronounced *sim*—letting his long robe fly in the air. The sound the drum emits is thought to inspire all animals with fur.

Mogeo

A *mogeo* is a fish-shaped instrument that is carved from a single piece of wood. Inside each *mogeo* is a wooden stick that is used to "play" it from the inside, and the sound is believed to resonate with all animals with scales. The instrument is also meant to serve as a form of admonition—that one must always strive to practice Buddhism like a fish that never closes their eyes. Operating with a similar level of symbolism, the *unpan* is an instrument made from bronze and shaped to look like a cloud. When played, it emits a sound that assists the awakening of all winged creatures that fly.

called pagoda in English after the Japanese name for the structure. There are other structures similar to pagodas, called *budo*, which contain the relics of eminent monks. Pagodas are normally located at the center of the temple because they represent truth. *Budos*, on the other hand, are placed on the edge of the temple precinct.

THE DAILY LIFE OF PRACTITIONERS

A day at a temple begins at 3 a.m., and everything is finished by 9 p.m.

This tradition is one that continues from the times of communal agriculture, but a temple dweller's morning arguably begins earlier than that of any other person—farmers included. Monks open their eyes before anyone else so that they can awaken all other beings. This ceremony is known as *doryangseok* and involves walking around the temple precinct while reciting the Buddha's name to the

Learning temple rules and basic temple etiquette

sound of *moktak* (a wooden instrument about the size of two fists). And just as *doryangseok* is over, the main worship of the Buddha begins.

Yebul is a ceremony that offers recitation of scriptures as an offering to the Buddha. It must be performed twice per day: once in the early morning and again in the evening. The morning *yebul* is specifically intended to be a prayer for all things that have just awoken, calling on them to follow the Buddha's teaching and escape eternal suffering. For a monk who has taken the tonsure (the shaving or close cropping of an area at the crown of one's head), this is a moment to affirm his or her will before the Buddha and bodhisattvas that they will do his utmost to perform their duties. Everyone who is a member of the temple must be present at the morning *yebul*, from the most senior monk to the youngest novice.

After *yebul*, the whole assembly will clean the temple inside and out. At a temple, each and every task in life constitutes practice and cleaning is no exception. According to an ancient saying, it is possible to tell how orderly a given temple is just by looking for the traces of sweeping in the temple courtyard. This physical labor, necessary even at a religious establishment such as a Buddhist temple, is called *ullyok*.

Once *ullyok* is finished, it is time for *gongyang*, whose original meaning was to making an offering to the Three Treasures of Buddhism: the Buddha, the Dharma, and Sangha (the monastic community). This offering was to be made with the body, the mouth (the equivalent of speech), and the mind (thought), but at Korean temples the word *gongyang* also refers to meals. In the past, breakfast would be gruel, lunch would be a full meal, and a light meal would be served at dinnertime. Nowadays, however, all three meals consist of rice and an assortment of side dishes.

One of the most important hours in the daily schedule of the temple is *sasi*, or 10 a.m. This is when a ceremonial offering of food is made to the Buddha. Known as *sasi* worship, or *maji*, this ceremony is modeled after the fact that lay Buddhists offered food to the Buddha and his disciples at this hour of the day.

Once *sasi* worship is over and the morning schedule comes to an end, it is time for the main practice to begin. Ordinarily, Korean Buddhist monks use meditation as their main method of practice. Depending on the temple, this practice can last for 2 to 3 hours per day, or up to 10 hours. During the twice-a-year seasonal retreat known as *angeo* (to take refuge), almost all monks will spend the majority of their time on practice only.

When the day's schedule is more or less over and the evening approaches, a worship session commences that is similar to that which happens in the early morning. Compared to the morning version that begins with *doryangseok* and lasts a relatively long time, the evening worship is a simpler affair. After this, a monk will use their time as they see fit or engage in additional prayers and practices, finishing the day at around 9 p.m.

Practice is an endeavor to fill oneself with positive energy and project that energy onto the surrounding area.
© Cultural Corps of Korean Buddhism

IMBUING EVERY GESTURE WITH ONE'S MIND

A temple is widely understood to be a religious establishment—a space where ceremonies are performed in accordance with religious conventions, and where people come to collect their thoughts. In Korean Buddhism, adhering to conventional etiquettes, especially inside the dharma hall, is very important. Bearing this in mind, there is no reason to be overly nervous or meek; given that temple spaces are open to everyone, the rules is considered necessary only to encourage harmony among visitors and prevent causing offense to one another.

Buddhism strictly distinguishes between monks and lay Buddhists. While monks live in accordance with the rules of the temple and observe them strictly, lay Buddhists do not need to follow such rules. Remembering some simple etiquette and a few basic matters of importance will often be sufficient, such as how to act within a temple, how to greet others, and how to eat. But be mindful that the most important thing is not to parade oneself and draw attention but rather to consciously aid the practice and prayers of others. Once you remember that fact, it is not so difficult to adhere to the basic etiquette and act in accordance with other rules.

Basics

It is not hard to follow the fundamentals of temple etiquette if one understands what a temple represents. The entryway, either the Iljumun or Haetalmun, serves to demarcate the world inside the temple enclosure from that which lies outside. The world outside the gate is where every being resides, and inside is the world of the Buddha. When you enter through this gate, bring your palms together in front of your chest and lightly bend your waist, performing a half-bow. It is a simple but effective gesture of respect.

Inside the temple there are several buildings. Among them, the most important space is the dharma hall, or Daeungjeon, where the main Buddha (often the historical Buddha Shakyamuni) is enshrined. The doors to Daeungjeon are located both in the front of the structure and at the sides, but be careful not to enter through the front doors that face the Buddha—these are reserved for monks. Lay Buddhists who have not taken the tonsure should use side doors. On entering the dharma hall, arrange your shoes neatly so that they point toward the outside, not inside.

The dharma hall is a space for worship and practice. For this reason, when you are in the dharma hall, you will see many people who are bowing to the Buddha. It is improper to walk in front of them as they bow. When walking inside the dharma hall, make sure not to make a loud noise with your heels, as the sound of your footsteps may disrupt others who are inside the building. In addition, walking around loudly can surprise and bother those who are attempting to practice in silence.

When inside the dharma hall, lighting candles is not only permissible but encouraged. Such offerings signal wholehearted devotion to the Buddha, as well as a desire for wish fulfillment. The incense also has the dual function of purifying both bad smells and evil influences, while the candles symbolize illumination of the world. But if you see that candles and incense are already lit, do not light new ones—this would be a waste. Extra candles or incense sticks that you have brought can simply be placed on the altar. When exiting the dharma hall, make sure to extinguish all the candles and incense; Korean temples are mostly made out of wood and thus very vulnerable to fire.

When walking around the temple grounds, place your left hand above your right so that they come together in front of you in the gesture known as *chasu*. The palms must face your body. Do not put pressure on the hands—simply maintain a light grip. *Chasu* has the effect of increasing one's humility and calming the mind.

Encountering a Monk

When meeting people inside the temple precinct, one does a half-bow with the palms together or a slight bend of the neck as a form of greeting. The same applies to meeting a monk. When meeting a monk in a more official setting, however, one should honor the custom of doing a triple prostration. A monk is a practitioner who dedicates their whole life to the pursuit of awakening and severing of all attachments, which means they also serve as teachers for all lay Buddhists who strive to attain awakening. That is why they deserve to receive the triple prostration. But if the monk is eating or practicing or lying on the floor, the triple prostration is unnecessary. It is also important to remember that one does not have to perform any greeting for a monk, even inside a temple, if it is before the early morning worship.

Some temples provide uniforms to temple stay participants.

Dressing

One of the most common questions people ask when they visit a temple for the first time is "What should I wear when I go to a temple?" People will sometimes visit a nearby temple on a whim during a journey and suddenly wonder, "Am I dressed too formally?" or "Am I dressed too comfortably?"

In short, one can wear any clothing that does not cause discomfort while doing the prostration and that does not make onlookers uneasy in the tightly shared space of the dharma hall. Meditation requires being seated for a long time, so it is necessary to wear comfortable clothes if this activity will be a part of your visit. Anything that clings to the body can cause discomfort to the wearer, and thus interfere with serious practice. This is particularly important in the summer, as improper clothing can not only distract one from meditation or prostration but also make others uncomfortable. Even if you are barefooted in your shoes, it is best to bring socks to put on before entering the dharma hall. In colder months, by contrast, it is against Buddhist precepts to wear any form of fur because Buddhism forbids killing. Hats are acceptable, but not inside the dharma hall.

Eating

Temple stays provide meals in accordance with the tradition of *barugongyang* Simply put, it is a method that uses food containers called *baru*, which means "an appropriately sized vessel." There are four *barus* given at mealtime: The biggest is for rice, the second is for soup, the third is for side dishes, and the final one is for water, with each bowl being smaller than the last. The rice bowl will be placed

to one's left, and the others will be placed in decreasing order of size in a counterclockwise direction.

Barugongyang is a practice that has continued since the time of the Buddha Shakyamuni and is more than simply a process for filling a hungry stomachm, it's is as much part of practice as worship or praying. It is considered a way to cleanse the mind, and it is important that one takes only what he or she can consume at the given meal, as it is disrespectful to leave any portion of your meal unfinished.

Before eating, be thankful for the food contained in your *baru*. Begin the meal with a mind full of gratitude for the efforts of those who made the food, as well as for the earth, wind, sun, and water. At this time, say a prayer. Recite *Ogwange*, or the verse of five contemplations.

> Where does this food come from? I am ashamed to receive it with my lack of virtue. I receive this food so I can discard all greed in my mind and use it as medicine for supporting my body and enacting truth.

Ogwange differs slightly from temple to temple, but the underlying meaning is the same everywhere: A human being, who eats life to sustain life, should discard pride and eat with gratitude and confidence. It is also a prayer that one will use the energy gained from the food to go on and commit good deeds.

When the meal is finished, use the water in your smallest bowl to wash the other bowls and then drink it. There should not be even a small particle of food left. This step is especially important because of the Buddhist belief in hungry ghosts (those who were greedy in life and are then punished in the afterlife): those unfortunate souls have throats that are so narrow that even a food particle as small as a grain of pepper powder will block them and cause suffering. To ensure that they do not suffer so, there should be no food left for them to take.

Hapjang is a formal way of greeting in a temple.

BASICS OF TEMPLE ETIQUETTE: HAPJANG AND JEOL

Among other practices that make temple life unique, a temple has its own specific way of greeting. It involves putting two palms together in front of the chest and tilting the body toward another person. This act is called *hapjang banbae*, and is the most common form of salutation, one that is used by monks and laity alike. The practice of bringing the two palms together with ten fingers open to each other is believed to have been a traditional custom of India.

Hapjang

Hapjang also refers to the bringing together of a scattered mind. It is meant to signal that the eyes, ears, nose, tongue, and skin—the five sense organs— are tamed through concentration so that they do not run amok under the influence of external stimuli. There is another interpretation suggesting that the posture of *hapjang* symbolizes peace because you cannot fight

Jeol

another while both hands are in contact. As a result, some believe that the *hapjang* posture is symbolic of harmony between oneself and others.

There is an additional form of etiquette called *jeol*, or prostration. By placing the whole body on the ground, you can discard your pride and express respect for others. If *hapjang* is an informal greeting that expresses horizontal human relations and equality between oneself and others, *jeol* expresses a more vertical relationship—a greeting that conveys one's respect for another being through the whole body. This is why one does the prostration before the Buddha in the dharma hall or before an eminent monk of tremendous virtue.

While performing *jeol*, begin to lower your body while maintaining *hapjang*. Eventually place your left hand down on the ground for support. Bring your right hand and two knees down as well before finally lowering your forehead to the point that it touches the floor. Finally, flip your hands up so that the palms are facing the ceiling and placed next to your head. This is the basic procedure of *jeol*. When doing the triple prostration, or 108- or 1,000-bow prostration, assume the *hapjang* posture at the end of each *jeol* and touch your forehead with your hands while still lying on the ground. This is known as *godurye*. When the *jeol* is finished, bring yourself back up in the reverse order of what has just been described.

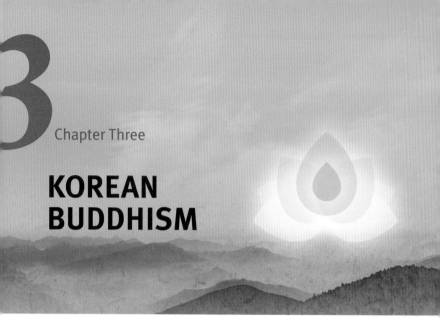

3
Chapter Three

KOREAN BUDDHISM

THE SEED OF BUDDHISM SPREADS IN KOREA

The origins of Buddhism lie in India, spurred when Prince Shakyamuni of the Kosala Kingdom, located in present-day Nepal, turned his back on all worldly attachments and left his home to pursue awakening. After six years of arduous practice, he attained nirvana under a Bodhi tree. As part of his enlightenment, he saw the formation and change of all things, as well as the complex knot of interdependent relations among all beings. He understood the truth of cause and effect in those relations, and illuminated the cause of all suffering that we experience due to reasons of life, aging, disease, and death. The awakening of the Buddha was not limited to elucidating the cause of suffering: Because he was able to see the cause, he also knew the way we could escape our fate.

For 45 years after attaining nirvana, the Buddha transmitted the essence of what he learned to people around the world. After he expounded the dharma for the first time in the deer park in Sarnath, India, numerous disciples took up his teaching. The tradition from the Buddha's teachings traveled to South Asia and led to the formation of the Theravada tradition of early Buddhism, and then crossed the Himalayas and reached China, further evolving into the Mahayana tradition, which literally translates as the Great Vehicle. Mahayana Buddhism became the foundation of esoteric Buddhism, also known as Vajrayana. As the various forms of Buddhism continued to spread, the dharma of the Buddha Shakyamuni went eastward, finally reaching Korea in 372 C.E.

Cheonbuljeon's 1,000 Buddhas (Daeheungsa Temple, Jeollanam-do) (left)
Preaching Assembly of Shakyamuni (The Buddhist hanging scroll), silk, Joseon Dynasty, National Museum of Korea (right)

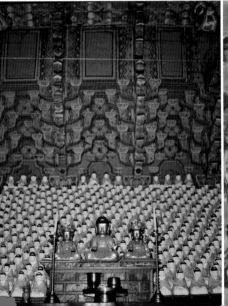 

The Awakening of the Buddha Continues in Korea

The most commonly accepted theory in academia is that Buddhism made its first appearance in Korea in the second year of the Goguryeo king Sosurim's reign (371–384). At that time the Three Kingdoms of Korea were preoccupied with trying to assert their supremacy over one another on the Korean Peninsula, though there is a record that Buddhism was officially introduced in 372 C.E. through the Former Qin Dynasty of China. According to this record, Emperor Xuanzhao (r. 357–385) of Former Qin sent monk Shundao (known as "Sundo" in Korean) with an emissary to Goguryeo. Shundao was carrying in his arms an image of the Buddha and Buddhist texts. This is the extent of the records available that can be objectively assessed and retold. But the record does not entirely show the full extent of the possible cultural exchange, as it is merely a state document. In fact, in a text titled The Liang Dynasty Biography of Eminent Monks, there are passages that suggest Buddhism had been transmitted to the Korean Peninsula before Shundao's arrival.

For this reason, it is difficult to say when Buddhism arrived in Korea exactly, but the year when Korea established its first Buddhist temple can be spoken of with more certainty. Seongmunsa Temple, also known as Chomunsa Temple, and Ibullansa Temple are the first Korean temples to be mentioned in writing.

The transmission of Buddhism can also be

Buddha with Inscription of "The Seventh Year of Yeonga," Goguryeo Kingdom (ca. 539), National Treasure No. 119, National Museum of Korea This statue is the oldest Buddhist sculpture with an inscribed date that has ever been found in Korea.

observed among the grassroots believers, the harbingers of change. While the exact year when Buddhism was officially adopted in Korea may not be known, Buddhism was already part of people's life long before that. Once a temple was able to gain official sponsorship, Buddhism became established as a foreign trend backed by the state. The record from the eighth year of the Goguryeo king Gogugyang (r. 384–391) shows that the king issued an edict: "Believe in and support the dharma of Buddhism and seek

Maitreya Bodhisattva at a temple site in Gunsu-ri, Baekje Kingdom, Treasure No. 330, National Museum of Korea. The wide face and full smile are characteristics of the Baekje-period statues.

fortune." Another record notes that in the following year, 392 C.E., the second year of King Gwanggaeto's reign, nine temples existed in Goguryeo's capital city, Pyeongyang. The establishment of these worship sites represented the culmination of a trend that would not be easily extinguished.

Goguryeo Buddhism was focused on scholasticism. Many monks who studied the doctrine through scriptures went to China with the goal of studying and researching various Buddhist texts. It is said that some of them attained a level of scholarship so high that they were able to teach Chinese monks. One of such scholars was Seungnang from the time of King Jangsu (r. 413–491). He devoted himself to the scholarship on Sanlun (*The Three Theories*, a series of texts in Chinese Buddhism), so much so that he was later able to formulate novel ideas about Sanlun, called *The New Three Theories*. His thoughts were taken up by monks such as Seungjeon, Beopnang, and Giljang, leading to the creation of an entirely new school of Buddhism called the Sanlun Order.

Baekje embraced this trend 12 years after

Goguryeo, a shift that happened during the kingdom's sole year under the rule of King Chimnyu (r. 384–385). An Indian monk named Malananta made the journey to Baekje to deliver the Buddhist message, travelling from Eastern Jin in China, and it is said that the king at the time welcomed the monk with open arms. Marananta built a temple in the Hansan region with royal sponsorship in 385 C.E. and trained Baekje's first 10 monks. Nearly a century and a half later, Baekje Buddhism reached its golden age under the 26th king, Seongwang (r. 523–554). Local religious leaders went so far as to have the entire set of Buddhist precepts brought back from India, and then translated and annotated. There is also a record that the king commanded the creation of an enormous Buddha statue and prayed for the awakening of all beings. They even transmitted Buddhism to another country: Baekje Buddhism went on to become the root of Japanese Buddhism, once the religion was transmitted there.

Baekje Buddhism focused on precepts, or a set of rules and principles. During the fourth year of King Seong's reign (r. 554–598), one of the ardent followers of the religion, Monk Gyeomik, went to India and learned Sanskrit while studying the precepts at the Sanggana Great Precept Temple (Nalanda monastery in India). Later, he returned home with Sanskrit versions of Abhidharma Pitaka (interpretations of the metaphysical dimensions of the Buddha's teaching) and a five-volume set of precepts

Pensive Bodhisattva, Three Kingdoms Period (Late 6th century), National Treasure No. 78, National Museum of Korea. This contemplative pose is quite common in Buddhist sculpture, and it was derived from the young Indian prince, Siddhartha Gautama, contemplating the nature of human life.

known as Obuyul. Back in Baekje, he translated 72 different texts that recorded various precepts with the assistance of 28 monks at Heungnyunsa Temple, playing a significant role in shaping Baekje Buddhism's distinct focus on precepts. Baekje's Buddhism also gave rise to a unique form of Buddhist art famous for its curved line aesthetic, the best example of this style being the gilt bronze statue of the bodhisattva Maitreya (pictured at left) in a seated posture.

Unlike Goguryeo and Baekje, which were proactive in receiving new cultural movements, Silla, by comparison, seems to have been more conservative, as Buddhism was not transmitted to Silla until several decades after Baekje first welcomed it. There are numerous hypotheses about the way in which Buddhism was adopted by the Silla kingdom, but common among many of them are references to a Goguryeo monk named Ado. There

Monument of Ichadon's Martyrdom in Heungryunsa Temple, Gyeongsangbuk-do

is no way to determine which hypothesis is true, unfortunately, except that while Goguryeo and Baekje accepted Buddhism through official diplomacy with China, Silla did not have such direct contact, at least not at the state level. It appears that in the process of Buddhism's transmission, there was much opposition due to the extremely insular tendencies of the ruling class.

What best illustrates the difficulty of this process is the martyrdom of Ichadon, which happened under the rule of King Beopheung (r. 514–540). The king wished to accept Buddhism as a state religion in order to strengthen royal authority, but the opposition from his officials was strong. At that time, Ichadon (503–527), a Buddhist, was martyred. At the heart of this incident were King Beopheung, who wished to strengthen royal authority by officially recognizing Buddhism to contain existing political forces, and Ichadon, who read the king's mind. Ichadon willingly sacrificed his life. It is recorded that when the executioner beheaded him at the king's order, a stream of white milk erupted instead of blood. This incredible occurrence led to the official recognition of Buddhism and its wide popularity in the Silla kingdom. It is thought that perhaps the white milk is a metaphor for the intensity of the experience among those who came into contact with the Buddha's teaching.

Using this dramatic event as a starting point, Silla Buddhism entered its gold age during the reign of King Jinheung (r. 540–576). By that time, the tonsure could be taken by anyone who so desired to, and even the king himself became a monk in his old age, taking a Buddhist name, Beopun—Dharma Cloud. A Buddhist name is similar to the name given after baptism in the Catholic Church: It signals one's commitment to and faith in Buddhism. King Jinheung's wife, the queen, also became a nun. During Jinheung's generation, a youth group founded on Buddhist thought was established for the purpose of cultivating young people's character. Hwarangdo, as this group was known, promoted the cultivation of the mind and body through Buddhist teachings, later playing an instrumental role in the unification of the Three Kingdoms. For this reason, one of the enduring attributes of Silla Buddhism is that of *hoguk*—nation protection.

The Flowering of Seon

Buddhism is largely divided into the Gyo Order, which studies the scriptures, and the Seon Order, which concentrates on the practical aspect of Buddhism known as Seon (Zen, in Japanese). If the Gyo Order strives to reach awakening by relying on the Buddha's recorded teaching and its interpretations, the Seon Order espouses a method that transcends the limitations of language and offers the experience of truth through one's own body.

To understand the circumstance under which Seon was introduced to Korea, one must first look at sixth-century China. At that time a figure named Bodhidharma (sometimes simply called Dharma) emerged on the Chinese Buddhist landscape. Though there are many theories and legends surrounding Bodhidarma's origins, many believe he was the third son of the king who ruled the kingdom of Xiangshi, located in present-day South India. After taking the tonsure he joined the lineage of Prajnatara, considered to be the upholder of a lineage going back to the Buddha Shakyamuni. After crossing into China he met the Liang Emperor Wudi and exchanged questions and answers with him. Next, he crossed the Yangzi River and climbed Mt. Song, where he did nothing for the next nine years except stare at a wall—engaging in "wall-staring meditation"—and transmitting the dharma to his disciple, Huike. This was how the Buddha dharma was transmitted from India to China.

Bodhidharma by Kim Myeong-guk (1600–unknown), Joseon Dynasty, National Museum of Korea

Dharma introduced Seon, which required examining one's mind, amid a climate of intense focus on a type of Buddhism centered on the scriptures. The goal of Seon is to see that the boundary between an ignorant being and an awakened Buddha is only that of a "single mind." It is to say that correctly seeing one's mind is more important than reading countless sacred texts. Everyone has a seed of Buddhahood within him or her, and this is called the

Buddha nature. Deep down, our true nature is this Buddha nature; Seon is to seek that Buddha nature.

Thus, the tradition of Seon that began with Dharma was continued by Huike, Sengchan, Daoxin, Hongren, and the Sixth Patriarch Huineng, under whom it flourished. Later, Seon was transmitted to Korea in the latter half of the Unified Silla Dynasty. It led to the opening of Nine Mountains of the Seon School, seen as the origin of Korean Seon Buddhism. Nine Mountains of the Seon School refers to the nine branches of the Seon Order that formed in late Silla and early Goryeo. They are Gaji, Silsang, Dongni, Heeyang, Bongnim, Seongju, Sagul, Saja, and Sumi.

Each branch of Korean Seon Buddhism has its root in the Seon Order established by Dharma. The lineage of Doheon, the monk who established Korea's Heeyang branch, is an offshoot of the Fourth Patriarch of Chinese Seon, Dosin. Other branches are heirs to the dharma of Mazu, who upheld the lineage of Huineng, the Sixth Chinese patriarch. These connections imply that the dharma of Korean Seon has completely absorbed the tradition of the Seon Order as initiated in China. Each Korean branch has gone on to produce its own distinct lineage and exceptional monks, meaning that the tradition of Seon that began in China has come into fruition through Korean Buddhism.

In the history of Korea's Seon Buddhism, the Nine Mountains occupy an extremely important position. At a time when the Gyo Order constituted the mainstream, the Nine Mountains exhibited very progressive tendencies and established themselves as centers of Seon practice. It is because of the Nine Mountains that the root of Seon in Korea could be made strong, eventually blossoming in the Goryeo Dynasty that followed.

The method of practicing Seon that began with early monks developed into two distinct forms of meditation: *mukjoseon* and *ganhwaseon. Ganhwaseon* in particular has established itself as the main form of practice in Korea following a pivotal moment in late Goryeo and continuing to this day. Having used to be considered as the exclusive preserve of monks and nuns, *Ganhwaseon* has recently been made accessible to the public. Now there exists a climate in which even lay Buddhists who have not taken the tonsure can routinely visit temples, urban missions, or Seon centers to participate in this practice. It would not be an exaggeration to say that Seon has become truly mainstream.

KOREAN BUDDHISM OVERCOMES DANGER AND RISES AGAIN

In tandem with Buddhism's arrival and its transformation under the Unified Silla and Goryeo Dynasties, the major ideas of Buddhism have had a sizable impact on the Korean Peninsula as a whole, ranging from everyday people's lives to the ruling ideology. A variety of approaches to life, culture, and art have developed through Buddhism, and Buddhist festivals like the Lotus Lantern Assembly and the Eight Precepts Assembly have become national events. Throughout this period, Korean Buddhism has achieved an unprecedented level of sophistication, exemplified in the Goryeo Buddhist paintings. The style was technically developed to the point that a single painting could feature countless nearly invisible Buddhas, and celadon vessels used in various Buddhist ceremonies were so refined in color and technique that they received international recognition. On the intellectual front, Buddhism absorbed characteristics of Theravada Buddhism as well as esoteric Buddhist ideas, forming a distinct system that had the values of Mahayana at its core.

During the Joseon Dynasty, however, Buddhism faced incredible danger. Until then, Buddhism had served as an unshakable ruling ideology, but in Joseon the system was forced to yield its position to

Confucianism; what had once been deeply embedded in the lives of people was gradually pushed out of the denser settlements and into the mountains. For 500 years thereafter, Buddhism was severely marginalized. Monks fleeing trenchant repression found themselves traveling from mountain to mountain for respite. By the end of the dynasty, the years of ongoing persecution had taken their toll on the very character of the religion, leaving it to absorb simplistic beliefs of the people such as praying for material gains.

It was amid this threat that a Buddhist monk Gyeongheo (1849–1912) appeared like a ray hope in late Joseon. He acquired his understanding of the principles of life and death by watching the people around him dying from pestilence. Through ceaseless practice he reopened the doors of Seon temples in the regions of Gyeongsang-do, Chungcheong-do, and Jeolla-do around 1900. The wind of Seon was about to blow once again.

But the tragedy facing Korean Buddhism was not yet over. No, this time Buddhism had to face the threat against not only itself but the whole nation: colonial rule. The history of modern Joseon was

Greeting the Soul of the Righteous Man on the Way to the Pure Land of Amitabha,
Tangut State of Hsi Hsia (12th–13th century), State Hermitage Museum, Russia (left)
Amitabha Triad, Goryeo Dynasty, National Treasure No. 218, Hoam Art Museum (right)

cruel indeed. It reached the point where language and writing, names, and even the root of Korea itself were about to be lost. In this difficult time, Seon masters focused purely on survival so that they could serve as pillars on which the whole nation could depend. In addition to Gyeongheo, there were other monks who also remained stoic during this difficult time, such as Yongseong, Hanyeong, Mangong, Hanam, and Manhae. Through ceaseless practice and dedication to the nation's independence, they safeguarded the lineage of Korean Buddhism and opened the door to a new era.

Among them, Yongseong, alongside Manhae, was one of the 33 national representatives who led the March 1 Independence Movement in 1919. He was a person who dreamed of national liberation and supported the independence movement, but he also occupies an important position in the history of Korean Buddhism. Yongseong laid the foundation that enabled modern Korean Buddhism to return to its original form after degenerating into a religion of worldly pursuits concerned only with fortune. He was also a pioneer in the translating of Classical Chinese scriptures into Korean so that many people could understand the Buddha's teaching. Looking to the future generations of Seon Buddhists, Yongseong successfully wrote Buddhist hymns, brought a harmonium into the temple, and created a choir. He can be seen as the initiator of a new proselytizing technique in modern Korean Buddhism.

The Japanese colonial occupation continued for 36 years, but when the long-awaited independence was achieved, it led to the national suffering of the Korean War. Between the 1950s and the early 1960s, the Buddhist Purification Movement (1954–1962) swept across the Buddhist establishment. Some parties have evaluated this action as a necessary process of purifying the order, which some felt had succumbed to widespread clerical marriage under Japanese rule. Others have deemed it rushed, saying that purification did not fully take into consideration what needed to be discarded and what was to be preserved.

There are some who still believe that Buddhism has not yet fully returned to its pure self, but history continues.

Korean Buddhism is still in the process of becoming a unified order. There have been many efforts to ensure that lay Buddhists will live a correct lay Buddhist life and monks a correct monastic one. The life of a Buddhist is attained through practice: This is what the Korean Buddhist establishment ultimately hopes to achieve. In the middle of all this was the master Seongcheol. Famous for saying that "A mountain is a mountain and water is water," Seongcheol played a critical role in continuing the tradition of *ganhwaseon* practice, embodying the archetype of a humble monastic while returning Buddhism from worldly concerns to its true nature.

Bongeunsa Temple, Seoul

Ganhwaseon: Speaking Words, Erasing Words

Ganhwaseon means to gaze at words, and it is a form of Seon practice that involves examining a specific type of speech. The practice is one that dwells on the conversation (called *hwa*, or more often *hwadu*) among eminent monks who have understood that the Buddha's wisdom leads to awakening. It is often called *chamseon*, and the mind must be fully engaged with the conversation during practice. Since it is mostly done in a seated position, it is also called *jwaseon*, but there is an additional walking type called *haengseon*. This practice, which China's Song Dynasty monk Zonggao systemized and disseminated, began with Bodhidharma and was divided into *mukjoseon* and *ganhwaseon*. From then on, several different orders accepted this practice method, causing it to undergo a more intricate evolution. Korean Buddhism appears to have accepted both methods, but in Korea the Seon practice was mostly developed as *ganhwaseon*, characterized by an intense, continuous focus on the meaning of particular phrases known as *hwadu*. In Korea, Jinul, also known as the National Master Bojo, was the

When you hear the sound of the bamboo clapper that a monk uses to signal the beginning of *chamseon*, you assume the lotus position by crossing your legs and direct your mind toward *hwadu*.
© Cultural Corps of Korean Buddhism

first to widely circulate this method. His leadership is why he is credited with being the founder of Chogyejong, or a patriarch responsible for the revival of Chogye in Korea.

Jinul was himself a practitioner of *ganhwaseon* and widely promoted it through his manifesto on what constituted correct Buddhist practice. From this point onward, the current of Korean Buddhism began to shift towards Seon, and *ganhwaseon* became known to be the surest way to reach awakening. This tradition of *ganhwaseon* practice begun by Jinul has come to be synonymous with Korean Buddhism, having survived through the religions history and continues to the present day.

It is said that once you understand *hwadu* in *ganhwaseon*, you discover that you yourself are a Buddha. This is called the Buddha nature, and because it is considered to be the same as seeing one's own nature, they use the expression *gyeonseong* or "seeing one's nature." Even if you do not discover your Buddha nature, the process of striving to claim it is practice in itself.

When you hear the sound of the bamboo clapper that a monk uses to signal the beginning of *chamseon*, you assume the lotus position by crossing your legs and directing your mind toward *hwadu*. It is a practice that requires concentration, and whenever there are wandering thoughts, you return your mind to the *hwadu*. *Haengseon* refers to focusing the mind on *hwadu* while walking.

The important part is to keep the eyes partially open so as not to fall asleep. Two hands should be lightly placed on the knees and the waist and back should be straight. Breathing is done through the nose. When you breathe in, breathe all the way down to the lower belly. Then breathe out through the nose. If you look sleepy or lose your proper posture, the monk will lightly hit your shoulder with the bamboo instrument. Among foreigners who are not familiar with *ganhwaseon*, this practice is commonly known as seated meditation, and *haengseon* is known as walking meditation.

The International Seon Center opened on November 15, 2010. Located in the Mokdong district of Seoul, the architectural design of the center was inspired by the nine-floor Hwangryongsa Temple of Gyeongju built during the Silla Dynasty. In the center, both locals an foreigners can experience the true essence of Korean Buddhism and *ganhwaseon* meditation through various temple programs.

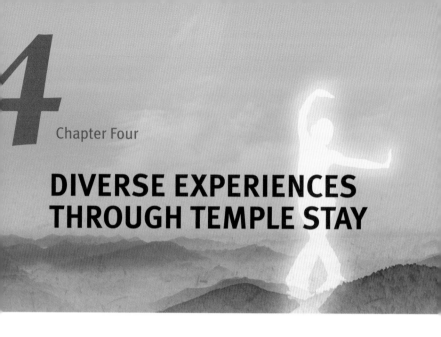

Chapter Four

DIVERSE EXPERIENCES THROUGH TEMPLE STAY

THE GROWTH OF TEMPLE STAY

Regardless of who you are, each day only has 24 hours. It always passes at the same rate. Nowadays, people will still try to split this limited time into fractions, putting off sleep so they can work more and dream of a better life: a more comfortable home; a better car; better-tasting food; better clothes. All of this requires pursuing money, which is seen as a guarantor of happiness. As a result, our minds have gone dry and we have lost the valuable time to reflect on ourselves. We are in desperate need of a pause like an oasis in a desert.

We have forgotten what truly matters because we are preoccupied with eating and living. But this pause has always been near us. The journey to a pause starts when you climb the beautiful mountains all over Korea. Mountainside temples will reveal the depth of

Korean Buddhist culture from the last 1,700 years when they hear the footsteps of visitors. Comprising one night at a temple not far from the city, temple stays have become the oasis for many who thirst for a break.

The purpose of a temple stay is to allow a person to experience Buddhism and the daily life of monks who practice it at traditional temples, places that embody Korean Buddhist culture. It is also a place where one can reexamine oneself and create new connections with monks, nature, and Korean Buddhism. Although temple stays have become this place of connection, they actually began as a form of lodging. The program dates back to 2002 during the World Cup games hosted by Japan and Korea, an event that saw Korea advance to the semi-final. The Korean government was worried about a lack of accommodation for foreign tourists and asked temples to open their doors—fortunately, Korean Buddhist temples obliged. The samething happened during the 2003 Summer Universiade Games.

Lotus flower tea

After the World Cup and the Universiade Games, temple stays became more than just means of accommodation. Foreigners singled out temple stays as the most memorable experience of their time in Korea, more so than the international events themselves. They appreciated the opportunity to experience Korea's living spiritual culture including worship, meditation, tea ceremonies, and glimpses of practitioners' lives. Therefore, in 2004, the Korean government designated temple stays as a national cultural resource and provided generous support.

Encouraged by positive reviews, Korean Buddhism developed cultural experience programs at various temples. Evolving from what used to be a simple itinerary—conversations with monks over tea, meditation, Buddhist meals, worship, and making lanterns—temple stays now encompass relaxation, rigorous practice, and culture and nature tours. Each temple has utilized its resources to the maximum,

The Templestay Information Center is located across the street from Jogyesa Temple, and can easily be accessed from Anguk Station or from Insa-dong Cultural Street. (eng.templestay.com)
© Cultural Corps of Korean Buddhism

Lotus lantern festival in Cheonggyecheon, Seoul

flavoring its temple stays with its natural surroundings and introducing programs as diverse as psychological healing, meditation, and temple cooking in order to offer more distinct and fun memories.

The rest format allows participants to freely select any activities according their wishes, while still making worship and Buddhist meals mandatory. Such activities include walking, hiking, and meditation. The practice format assigns a larger portion of the time to purely Buddhist practice. The culture and nature tour format allows closer contact with the surrounding environment. It offers activities such as natural dying, stele-rubbing (making rubbings of ancient inscriptions), trail walking, trekking, and the simple experience of being in a forest. The custom format is conducted in accordance with the wishes of the corporation or organization that requests such a service.

Temple stay programs grew rapidly as the roster of programs increased and diversified. Participation steadily increased, and by the 10th anniversary of the temple stay program in 2012, some 1.9 million people had experienced Korean Buddhist culture through

In 2011, the director-general of UNESCO, Irina Bokova, visited Bulguksa Temple and Seokguram Grotto in Gyeongju. © Beopbo Sinmun

the program. The demand came not just from within Korea but around the world. In 2002, there were only 1,300 foreign participants in temple stay programs; since 2008, the number has increased to 20,000 each year.

More than 40 people from 71 countries came to Korea to participate in the 2011 Miss Asia Pacific World Competition Korea and experienced temple stay. That same year, the director-general of UNESCO, Irina Bokova, visited Bulguksa Temple and Seokguram Grotto in Gyeongju, participating in hitting the *beomjong*, making rubbings off stone steles, and creating lotus lanterns. Afterward, she remarked, "It is incredible that a program that combines all these different experiences in an enjoyable format exists," adding, "It is a rare experience to be able to stay inside such great traditional cultural heritage sites."

The temple stay initiative, which embodies both Korean Buddhist culture and Korean spiritual culture, has been receiving high marks on the international stage. It won the best prize in 2008 and 2009 at the International Tourism Bourse, an event that draws participation from some 180 countries around the world. And in 2009, the Organization for Economic Cooperation and Development (OECD) designated that, in addition to being a global tourism resource that represents Korean culture, temple stays are also one of the world's "five most successful tourism products." The Korean government also selected the temple stay experience as one of the ten representative icons of Korea.

Since the program's inception, the global media have lavished praise on the temple stay initiative, with National Geographic Magazine naming temple stays as the most competitive cultural products worldwide and the U.S. News and World Report selecting temple stays as one of the 50 ways to contribute to having a "Healthy Mind."

Serving as a journey of happiness and self-discovery over one special night at a mountain temple, temple stays have been firmly established as a respite for urbanites in search of well-being and healing.

American actor Richard Gere holds a piece of clothing for his temple stay after he received it as a present from Ja-seung, the executive chief of the Korean Buddhist Jogye Order, upon his visit to the Jogyesa Temple in Seoul, 2011.

TEMPLE STAY INFORMATION AT A GLANCE

The Cultural Corps of Korean Buddhism has been utilizing global marketing through information technology to advertise temple stay programs around the world.

An English-language temple stay app for iPads

In 2011, it launched the first temple stay app, as well as a separate app just for tablet PCs. The iPhone app consists of four pages: the definition of what a temple stay is and represents, an etiquette guideline, information on participating temples, and a gallery. It can be used in English, and also features videos of nearby tourist attractions for maximum utility. The Temple Stay App Book in Korean and English is available for iPads and tablet PCs and features content that is similar to that which is available on smartphone applications. It offers a good look at the temple stay experience through photographs, videos, and guided explanation.

The Temple Stay Facebook page has also received a positive response both domestically and abroad.

The Cultural Corps of Korean Buddhism publishes and distributes English-language brochures that introduce the temple stay concept, as well as using its home page to share the latest news about temple stay programs, temple food, Buddhist cultural products, information centers, and customer service centers. You can search for participating temples in any region in the country, from Seoul, Gyeonggi-do, Incheon, Gangwon-do, Gyeongsangbuk-do, Gyeongsangnam-do, Chungcheongbuk-do, Chungcheongnam-do, Jeollabuk-do, Jeollanam-do, and even Jejudo Island.

- The temple stay home page: www.templestay.com
- The Cultural Corps of Korean Buddhism: www.kbuddhism.com

THE TEMPLE STAY PROGRAM FOR FOREIGNERS

An Enjoyable Experience for the Body and Mind

The temple stay program offers an experience of Korean Buddhist and spiritual culture. There are an increasing number of foreigners who come to Korea for various reasons and experience a temple stay, only to have their eyes opened to the appeal of both Buddhism and Korean traditional culture.

One French student who is deeply immersed in K-pop visited Korea on a Korean Wave–related tour and participated in a one-night stay at Jeondeungsa Temple in Ganghwa, Incheon. She calmed her busy mind through worship and meditation, and was able to learn the spiritual culture of Korea by doing 108 prostrations and walking meditation. There were few inconveniences for her as a foreigner because the temple was specially equipped to host foreign guests. Of the experience, she said, "I had deep respect for the monks who wake up in the early morning hours every day to practice."

Drying tea leaves © Cultural Corps of Korean Buddhism

Outdoor meditation

Tea ceremony

For a Canadian travel agent who has been to many places, the temple stay experience was equally memorable. The days he spent at Seonunsa Temple in Gochang, Jeollabuk-do, have left a deep impression on his mind. Among the various temple practices he encountered, he said he was particularly moved by the traditional temple dining method—*barugongyang*—and its lack of wastefulness, as well as the quiet atmosphere of the temple. Seonunsa Temple, too, specializes in temple stays for foreigners, so it was not difficult for him to make conversation with other visitors. "When I go back to Canada, I want to develop a travel product related to offering temple stays," he said. "I was profoundly influenced by the conversation I had with a monk over tea."

A French media figure reflected upon the experience of meditation in Korea, saying, "It left a lasting impression that made the long duration of concentration and breathing seem short."

One American journalism student visited Myogaksa Temple in Seoul in search of a temple stay program and said that she was constantly impressed by what she found. Having completed a one-day program called "Temple Life," she confessed, "After hearing the words of the monk, I realized that I needed to control my emotions, which tend to be dominated by the dissatisfaction and stress brought on by living a busy life."

Temples That Offer Programs for Foreigners

Language is not an issue in experiencing Korea's spiritual culture, Buddhism. There are many temples that can communicate with foreign participants in different languages. Throughout Korea there are about 20 temples that specialize in temple stays for foreigners, and all have specialized staff to assist guests with the experience. The Cultural Corps of Korean Buddhism, the organization that oversees temple stay programs, is operating programs for foreigners in Seoul, Incheon, Busan, Daegu, Gochang, Pyeongchang,

茶香四流

A conversation with monks

Hapcheon, Haenam, Gimje, Jeju, and other areas. They all use English as the main language of communication.

In Seoul there is the Mokdong International Seon Center, Geumseonsa Temple, Myogaksa Temple, and Bongeunsa Temple. Outside Seoul, many temples around the country offer programs directed at foreigners: Beomeosa Temple in Busan, Donghwasa Temple in Daegu, Seonunsa Temple in Gochang, Magoksa Temple in Gongju, Mihwangsa Temple in Haenam, Beopjusa Temple in Boeun, Yongjusa Temple in Hwaseong, Woljeongsa Temple in Pyeongchang, Jeondeungsa Temple in Ganghwa, Geumsansa Temple in Gimje, Jikjisa Temple in Gimcheon, Haeinsa Temple in Hapcheon, Golguksa Temple in Gyeongju, Hwaeomsa Temple in Gurye, Naesosa Temple in Buan, and Yakcheonsa Temple on Jejudo Island.

Temples that operate programs for foreigners are evaluated and selected based on a number of criteria including program plans, foreign-language abilities, exclusive staff for managing the program, marketing, and the surrounding environment. Unless there are staff who can handle one-on-one communication with foreigners, the temple cannot be selected for the category. It is necessary that program coordinators can speak foreign languages as well as understand Buddhism. This is the reason why foreigners can experience a temple stay without too much difficulty.

Basic Programs That Embody Korean Spiritual Culture

Temples that cater to foreigners offer the same basic programs offered to Koreans. They involve *chamseon* (meditation), tea ceremonies, monastic meals, lotus lantern–making, and threading prayer beads while reciting the 108 prostrations.

Chamseon refers to time spent simply looking at one's own mind while sitting on a floor cushion. The term literally translates as "cultivating Seon," and differs from meditation as conventionally

Threading 108 beads as one prostrates 108 times is also popular.

understood in the West. For this reason, it is sometimes replaced with more conventional meditation exercises in programs intended for foreigners. *Chamseon* involves concentrating, keeping extraneous thoughts at bay, and quietly calming the mind. For those seeking a different kind of reflective practice, conversations with monks can be arranged, typically taking place over a cup of tea. These can be an opportunity to reevaluate one's life and share with a monk the ailments of the mind.

Threading 108 beads as one prostrates 108 times is also popular. It is a practice that allows one to let go of the thought that "I am the best" and that "I am the most important person in this world." With each prostration, a single wooden bead will be placed on a thread, each time marking a decrease in one's selfishness. The resulting prayer beads can be taken as a token of the time one spent reexamining one's humbler self.

The lotus is a flower that symbolizes Buddhism because it blooms beautifully and cleanly out of muddy water, unsullied by the filthiness of mud. For this reason, temple stay programs offer a chance to make lotus lanterns by pasting thin paper petals in a flower pattern on a cup until the lotus bloom is complete.

Many foreigners have already had an experience at one of the country's diverse temple stay programs and become enamored with the lasting impression they provide. In 2008, some 20,000 people experienced temple stays, a number that has been surpassed in every year since then. All who have sought out a Korean temple experience have rated temple stays very highly.

The lotus is a flower that symbolizes Buddhism because it blooms beautifully and cleanly out of muddy water, unsullied by the filthiness of mud.

According to a survey carried out by the Cultural Corps of Korean Buddhism, foreigners have given the temple stay experience a score of 8.6 out 10 for general satisfaction. Out of every 10 participants, 9 said they would recommend it to other people. What is the reason? For the most part, they were especially satisfied with the tea ceremony, prayer beads– and lantern-making, and conversations with monks. They gave a satisfaction rating of 8 or higher on the same scale for most activities including conversations with monks (8.60), lotus lantern– and prayer beads–making (8.57), 108 prostrations (8.55), walking meditation (8.32), and *chamseon* (8.26).

EXPERIENCE BUDDHIST TEMPLE CULTURE TO OPEN UP YOUR MIND

Barry James Anderson / English Teacher

I had been attending the weekly meditation sessions and dharma talks at the Seoul International Seon Center at Hwagyesa Temple in northern Seoul for about a month when I came across a brochure for Musangsa Temple. My vacation from work was coming up and shortly thereafter I had already booked my return flight to Canada. I remember thinking that I found this brochure just in time. But when I realized that I had to participate in the retreat for a minimum of seven days, I questioned if my creaking knees and back could take it. However, I decided that a "now or never" approach was appropriate and I signed up soon afterward.

Musangsa turned out to be just what I had hoped for: a quiet and serene temple perched on the side of Mt. Gyeryongsan overlooking rice paddies and farmers' fields, far away from the noise and bustle of Seoul. After a helpful orientation session, newcomers were given gray robes to wear during the duration of our stay. Before I knew it, my retreat had begun.

I must admit the first few 3:00 a.m. wake ups didn't come so naturally, but after a couple of days I found the sound of a monk chanting while playing a *moktak* to be vastly preferable to the beeping alarm clock I was accustomed to. After a quick wash of the face, the day started with 108 full prostrations. Despite seeming to take forever during the first day or two, the bows became enjoyable rather quickly. Morning and evening chants were some of the most appreciated periods of the retreat schedule. I am not sure if it was the rare opportunity to use my voice or the energy that seemed to be generated during the chanting, but regardless, I could not deny feeling more positive afterward. The meals were intimidating at first: During breakfast and lunch, eating is done in a formal way with a set of four bowls, each with a specific function and significance. After the initial dining room jitters wore off, I started to notice how delicious and fresh the food was. Meals were eaten in silence, and the effect of this is that you actually pay attention to what you are eating instead of munching away while watching TV, reading a newspaper, or doing something else to occupy your mind. Another rule followed in the dining room is that you must finish all of the food that you take, wasting nothing. This action exemplifies the simple relationship of cause and effect very clearly; careless over-indulgence when serving oneself will inevitably lead to suffering. It is very basic, but how often in our day do we stumble along in a trance of sorts, oblivious to the outcome of actions we are constantly taking?

Aside from the bowing, chanting, meals, and a one-hour work period, the days were filled with meditation sessions in the dharma room. Sitting meditations were usually done in two- or three-hour blocks consisting of 30–40 minutes of sitting or standing, alternated with 10 minutes of walking meditation. I soon learned how difficult it was to slow down the mental multitasking I had spent 25 years practicing. When sitting on a cushion facing a white wall, I was almost forced to observe the frequency and arbitrariness of the various thoughts and urges that popped into my mind. My desires and feelings came and went, involving everything from my upcoming travel plans to what I was hoping would be served for dinner. I asked the abbot of the temple what I should do when I simply couldn't get away from my thinking. His answer was simple; he explained that our true self or original self, or whatever you choose to call it, is like the clear blue sky. Thinking and desires are like clouds floating through, obscuring the sky. Sometimes there are lots of clouds, and sometimes not so many, but if you are patient and simply watch the clouds without trying to push them out, then the situation will take care of itself. I took those words to heart and devoted the rest of my stay at the temple to "cloud watching."

Other parts of the Musangsa Temple Stay schedule included weekly interviews with the abbot, Monk Mushim, and Sunday dharma talks. The interviews were a little unnerving at first, but the warm demeanor of Monk Mushim quickly put me at ease. Monk Mushim is originally from America, but relocated to Korea to follow his teacher, Monk Seung Sahn. He was more than willing to answer questions concerning nearly anything, and did so with consideration and kindness. The Sunday dharma talks were given by one of the resident monks and then questions were taken by Monk Mushim. When you spend most of your day simply sitting in a cross-legged position, a few wise words go a long way. However, the best part of staying at Musangsa Temple was that the schedule is set, so all you have to do is follow the situation, try, and be patient.

I have returned to Musangsa Temple for three more retreats since that first crash course in Seon meditation, and each time I found the experience rewarding, though in different ways. The temple staff and resident monks are friendly and eager to help in any way possible, be it with travel arrangements, medical concerns, or simple questions about experiences in the meditation room. I have truly appreciated my time at Musangsa Temple and recommend it as a direct way to experience both the natural beauty of Korea and also the time-honored tradition of Korean Buddhism.

FROM MARTIAL ARTS TO COFFEE BEANS: SPECIAL TEMPLE STAY PROGRAMS

Temple stay programs for foreigners offer various intriguing programs. You can learn a martial art and walk along a path through a thousand-year-old fir forest. But even if you do not go to a temple that specifically caters to foreigners, you can experience more unique programs simply by contacting the right temple in advance and inquiring about particular activities.

Golgulsa Temple: The Birthplace of Sunmudo

Golgulsa Temple in Gyeongju (www.sunmudo.com) has gained international fame for its *sunmudo* training, sought out by foreigners who want to study Korean Buddhist and traditional

Sunmudo uses basic martial arts maneuvers and movements to examine one's mind.

martial arts. In 1992, it officially began offering a program under the temple stay structure.

Sunmudo is a way of disciplining the mind and body for monk practitioners, a traditional martial art that has continued through the Silla, Goryeo, and Joseon Dynasties. It is said that Hwarang, an organization created by King Jinheung of Silla to locate talented individuals, created 12 caves on Mt. Hamwolsan—where Golgulsa is located—and used them to practice martial arts. In Joseon, warrior monks practiced their arts here. *Sunmudo*, which has been a traditional method of Buddhist practice for a long time, is a systematic martial art that allows the mind, body, and breathing to come into harmony and leads to awakening. It was discontinued during Japanese colonial rule, but a persistent monk by the name of Yangik restored the tradition at Beomeosa Temple in Busan, and the current abbot of Golgulsa, Jeogun, has since turned it into the representative martial art of Korea.

The *sunmudo* temple stay offered at Golgulsa teaches participants

Walking around the forest surrounding Woljeongsa Temple, Gangwon-do, is enough to bring serenity to the mind.

the art of *sunmudo* and trains them vigorously on a quiet mountain. Each day begins and ends with *sunmudo*. After breakfast, participants engage in a form of yoga—this being a component of *sunmudo*—and a qigong practice that circulates qi (energy) through the whole body. Next come the 108 prostrations that provide a chance to look back at one's stagnant life and atone for it. After lunch comes a number of small tasks requiring manual labor (*ullyeok*), such as sweeping the temple grounds and pulling out weeds alongside the monks—a chance to learn the importance of hard work with one's hands. After dinner, one engages in more intensive *sunmudo* training.

Sunmudo uses basic martial arts maneuvers and movements to examine one's mind. Using Seon calisthenics, which comprise 18 different movements, one relaxes one's stiff muscles and examines the flow of energy within oneself. It is then followed by 12 different movements that are modeled on the forms of seven different animals, such as dragon, monkey, and deer, and then ends with a posture that expresses the awakening of the Buddha. It is not a martial art meant for attacking others, so if you joined the program thinking you would be learning the skills from martial arts films, you will be sorely disappointed.

The Golgulsa temple stay offers one additional attraction: One should not miss seeing the Rock-carved Seated Buddha at Golguram Hermitage (Treasure No. 581), or making a pilgrimage to a rock façade where various shrines of small Buddhas are created out of small holes that are both naturally occurring and artificially made.

Woljeongsa Temple: Walking a Path through a Thousand-Year Fir Forest

The temple stay program at Woljeongsa Temple in Pyeongchang, Gangwon-do, is healing, pure and simple. Woljeongsa (www. woljeongsa.org) is located at Mt. Odaesan, which is famous for its blessed nature.

The area where Woljeongsa Temple is located is called "Happy 700," as the region's elevation—700 m above sea level—is apparently considered ideal for human inhabitation. Therefore, just walking around the forest surrounding Woljeongsa Temple is enough to bring serenity to the mind. The practice of doing walking meditation through the fir forest is the most popular temple stay program among foreigners and Koreans alike. The unpaved road through the fir forest is famous among those who wish to do the three-step, one-prostration practice, as it teaches people to let go of their egoes and return to the principle of nature.

There is also an old road called Seonjaegil that leads to a rest area on the Odae Mountain Lodge, followed by Sangwonsa Temple. Over the course of the trail's 10 kilometers, you can feel the dirt path with your bare feet and dip your feet in a stream. Woljeongsa Temple has restored much of the course, using rocks and other materials to create passages over the area's streams so that participants can truly feel as though they are part of nature.

Another advantage of Woljeongsa's temple stay program is Jeokmyeolbogung (the Treasure Palace of Nirvana), which contains bone fragments of the historical Buddha collected after the cremation of his body. From Woljeongsa Temple, you pass Sangwonsa and continue walking for two or three hours through the forest past a hermitage to reach Jeokmyeolbogung. It is one of five such structures in Korea, and many pilgrims come to visit this site specifically. If you want to take in a more unique temple stay experience, you can try walking to the palace while performing the three-step, one-prostration practice.

Naksansa: A Place to Cast One's Worries into the Blue East Sea

If you do not like mountains, another option is to go to the sea. Naksansa (www.naksansa.or.kr) in Yangyang-gun, Gangwon-do, is a temple popular among those who want to listen to the sound of waves while relaxing next to the East Sea. Their temple stay program "Follow the Way to a Dream" is the very definition of the rest format, offering a two-day, one-night itinerary that does not push participants to commit to too many activities. You can freely choose from different options such as going to the East Sea, viewing the sunset, *ullyeok* (carrying out small chores), *chamseon* (meditation), reading, and prayer. Naksansa also features spaces with traditional architectural details intended for temple stay guests, allowing one to experience comfortable rest and leisure.

The rest-format temple stay programs only expect that participants join the morning and evening worship sessions, as well as monastic meals. Besides keeping those appointments, one can spend his or her time freely inside the temple precinct. It is an

The famous 16-meter statue of the bodhisattva Avalokitesvara in Naksansa Temple, Gangwon-do

Hongyeon-am pavilion in Naksansa Temple

especially popular program among urbanites who seek out quiet rest and time for self-examination instead of a busy and loud summer vacation.

Naksansa's more practice-driven overnight-stay program, "Asking about the Road While on the Road," is more focused on activities traditionally associated with temple stays: 108 prostrations, *chamseon*, walking meditation, and sunrise viewing in front of the temple's famous 16-meter statue of the bodhisattva Avalokitesvara. There is also a weekend program called "In Search of a Bluebird" that consists of monastic meals, walking meditation, and "mind sharing" in lieu of 108 prostrations and *chamseon*. It has gained much popularity among participants.

There is also a more experience-oriented program called "Mandala Meditation." Over two nights and three days, participants learn about the basic concept and structure of a mandala (a diagram depicting truth) and form teams with others to create one out of sand. The process of making a mandala and expressing one's dreams and wishes through it has received a positive response from those who have participated in the program.

Each of the programs offered at Naksansa Temple are announced on the site's homepage, so it is important to check for dates and availability before planning a visit. Registration begins one month before the program date, and is possible up to one week before the start of the session. Foreigners can participate in any program alongside Koreans.

Hyeondeoksa: Savory Healing through Coffee

If you go to Gangneung, Gangwon-do, the only place in Korea with a coffee festival, a coffee museum, and a coffee street, you can experience a temple stay program with a bit of a coffee flavor. Hyeondeoksa (www.hyundeoksa.or.kr) has a program that beckons the sounds of waves, birds, and bells, while also offering the fragrance of coffee. The session runs over the course of one day and is offered regularly. In addition to meditation, drawing, walking, trekking, making prayer beads, and painting fans, you can also choose to roast and grind your own fresh coffee beans to make drip coffee.

This distinct program, which mixes both temple and coffee culture, owes its existence to the abbot of the temple, Hyeonjong,

In Gangwon-do, Hyeondeoksa Temple's "Coffee Roasting Time" is currently attracting much enthusiasm from participants.

who started to offer temple stay participants coffee made from beans he himself roasted. One might think that monks and coffee do not mix, but Hyeonjong explains that while Eastern practitioners drink tea to clear their minds, Western practitioners drink coffee.

The special experience of drinking coffee made from beans roasted by a monk at this temple has become famous through word of mouth, causing more people to begin visiting Hyeondeoksa Temple. As a result, the temple began presenting a program titled "Coffee Roasting Time" among their temple stay offerings. As you select coffee beans and roast them, you can reflect on your own life and the warmth of coffee served in the traditional teacups Hyeondeoksa uses. The temple's "Coffee Roasting Time" is currently attracting much enthusiasm from participants.

Gapsa: Meeting a Summer Waterfall at Its Peak

Mt. Gyeryongsan is considered to be the most auspicious site on the Korean Peninsula. It is famous for its autumn, waterfall, and temple stay programs at Gapsa (www.gapsa.org), with the temple stay attracting many people from both inside and outside Korea.

The number of foreign participants is increasing rapidly, including such participating countries as France, Russia, Norway, Italy, England, and Germany. The program will sometimes attract up to 100 visitors from continental Europe at the same time, filling all of the program spots very quickly.

The beautiful scenery of Gapsa in autumn is considered to be among the best in Korea, leading some to call the temple Chugapsa—Autumnal Temple. In reality, however, Gapsa's temple stay program is best enjoyed in the summer. One reason for this is Yongmun Pokpo, or the Dragon Gate Waterfall, and another is a nearby stream that will wash away all of the concerns accumulated in your mind and body. The water of the stream is crystal-clear, calming and purifying participants' minds, and the majestic sound of the Dragon Gate Waterfall is thunderous to the point of allowing concentration deep enough to transcend time. While listening to the sound of the waterfall, participants will let go of greed and enter the path of healing. Last year, one participant who spent a summer night at Gapsa said, "The sound of water and wind at the Dragon Gate Waterfall allowed me to let go of the idea of 'me' and greed, thus permitting me to accept the sound of nature.... It taught me the simple truth that hearing comes before myself, who had always thought only of putting my own point of view first."

Yongmun Pokpo, or Dragon Gate Waterfall, Chungcheongnam-do

Gapsa's temple stay is an opportunity to surrender custody of "me" to the beautiful and pure slopes of Mt. Gyeryongsan and pay heed to the resonance of one's interior and nature—letting go of speed, which symbolizes infinite competition, and adjusting oneself to the rhythm of nature leads to slowness. The temple staff has recently created other programs that offer an experience of Buddhist culture characteristic of Baekje's spirit.

Besides engaging in *chamseon* at the Dragon Gate Waterfall, participants can enjoy the scenery; meditate on a forest path; make ceramics, lanterns, and prayers beads; perform calisthenics; and do many other activities that marry traditional culture with natural beauty. All the programs offer the gift of leisure to one's inner self, who feels constantly chased by daily obligations of life.

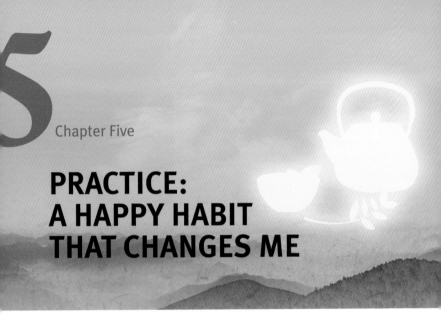

Chapter Five

PRACTICE: A HAPPY HABIT THAT CHANGES ME

Buddhism is often called the religion of practice, referring to how central a role that practice plays in Buddhism; without it, the religion is only half complete. Practice—also known as cultivation—embodies efforts to change the mind behind words and actions in a more positive direction. It is an endeavor to fill oneself with positive energy and project that energy onto the surrounding area. This a continuous tradition with a 2,500-year history since the Buddha Shakyamuni first attained awakening in India.

That longstanding tradition has reemerged as a new solution in the history of humanity. The practice of cultivating a more positive mind with less desire and more contentment is now being introduced as a way to resolve the poverty of the mind amidst abundance of our materialistic civilization.

Korean Buddhism has carried out various practices such as *ganhwaseon*, *yeombul*, *gangyeong*, *dokgyeong*, *sagyeong*, *jeol*, and *vipassana* for the last 1,700 years. Recent scientific studies have revealed and demonstrated their effectiveness.

This chapter introduces the way practice changes our lives, the practices in Korean Buddhism and their methods, and practices that can be done easily.

A PRACTICE THAT HEALS THE BODY AND MIND

Practice is a way to let go of the thought that oneself is the best. So when you meet monks who have been practicing, you might be moved by their warm speech and demeanor. You may even develop respect for their positive energy and try to emulate them. This happens because monks have let go of their preoccupation, stubbornness, preconception, and sense of superiority that once filled themselves.

Why are monk practitioners so serene? It is because their mind and body are healthy. As society as a whole beings to pay more attention to the health of the mind and body, the practice of Korean Buddhism is also gaining much attention. *Ganhwaseon* has been shown to be effective in the fields of therapy and neurology. A Buddhist publication called the *Beopbo Sinmun* recently reported on the average lifespan of 67 eminent monks who represent Korea and China. Their average lifespan was determined to be 76.6 years, and 60 of them had lived past the age of 60. Because these monks lived during a time when medicine was relatively under-developed, this fact—that they had lived a similar lifespan as most people do today—caused shock and many began asking about their secret.

The medical community focused on the fact that it is possible to control stress through *chamseon*, which reduces anxiety caused by emotional changes in response to environmental factors as well as anxiety due to one's preexisting tendencies. There are also reports that *chamseon* can stimulate the production of serotonin in the brain and calm the mind, and apparently also

stimulates the production of the alpha wave normally generated in the state of relaxation and rest. One professor who has studied this question extensively at Ilsan Hospital of Dongguk University said in one article that *chamseon* reduced the production of stress hormones such as cortisol and adrenalin and increased the blood flow and oxygen supply to the brain, as well as serotonin production. Another professor who specializes in psychology and has researched the relationship between heart beats and Buddhist practice argues that *chamseon* can slow down the heart and reduce unnecessary energy expenditure, thus bringing about a decrease in anxiety.

There is a monk who has taken advantage of the fact that *chamseon* can have a positive effect on the body and the mind. Monk Seogwang has created a special program for psychological healing that utilizes *chamseon*. He leads the Korea Institute for Meditation and Psychological Counseling and has introduced a program called "Recovering the Human Mind." It is a method for controlling the ego and the pattern of repetition behind habitual and negative reactions in the mind, as well as cultivating an awareness of one's feelings and thoughts.

Briefly put, the method involves three things: stopping, breathing, and asking. In the throes of suffering, briefly stop your action, take several deep breaths, and put a hand on the chest and ask oneself, "Who am I?," "Where was my mind before my present state of mind?," "Where will my mind go after this moment?," and "Is this really the way for me to truly care for people that I hold dear?" With such questions, you let go of your suffering and fill your mind with positivity.

Even if you have no intention of doing any practice, these questions as posed by the "Recovering the Human Mind" therapy can be good things to ask of oneself—good cures for an ailing mind.

TYPES AND METHODS OF PRACTICE IN KOREAN BUDDHISM

Korean Buddhism offers various forms of practice. They include *ganhwaseon*—tireless meditation on the conversations among great masters of the past—as well as invocation of the Buddha (*yeombul*), incantation (*juryeok*), silent reading (*gangyeong*) and chanting (*dokgyeong*) of the scriptures, and prostration (*jeol*) among others. *Yeombul* means single-mindedly reciting the Buddha's name in a mental state free of distractions, and *juryeok* involves chanting the true words of the Buddha (for example, "Om mani padme hum"), also known as incantations, in a rhythmic, loud voice as if they were songs.

Transcribing the scriptures character by character with a devotional mind and applying ink to a panel and printing the scriptures page by page also constitute forms of practice in Korean Buddhism.

The prostration of the whole body, too, is a Buddhist practice when it is done as 108; 1,000; 1,080; 3,000; or 10,000 bows with the purpose of atoning for one's faults. In addition, a form of mindfulness meditation known as *vipassana* has recently gained much popularity in Korea as another kind of practice.

The hand positioning of the Bonjonbul is known as *hangmachokjiin*. This Buddhist position was used by Seokgamoni upon being tempted by the devil as he sat on the brink of enlightenment.

Yeombul: Calling the Buddha

Yeombul—literally, "reflecting on the Buddha"—involves reciting the Buddha's name, and it is the most common form of Buddhist practice in Korea. It has existed since the beginning of Buddhism under the name of Buddhanussati as a practice of contemplating the meanings embedded in the 10 names of the Buddha, such as the Arhat and the World-Honored One.

Yeombul has developed in Korean Buddhism because of the belief that there are different Buddhas not only in our world but also in many other worlds around the cosmos. *Yeombul* should be considered as an oath to follow the will of the Buddha, sworn on the names of many enlightened beings such as the Buddha Amitabha and the bodhisattvas Avalokitesvara and Ksitigarbha. Scriptures note the benefits of *yeombul* as increased ecstasy and

Buddhist prayer beads

happiness, a victory over anxiety and fear, and a feeling of being in the presence of the Buddha.

There are three ways of doing *yeombul*: *chingmyeong yeombul*, which is done aloud; *gwanneom yeombul*, which is done without any sound; and *yeombulseon*—the invocation of the Buddha as a meditative practice. Ordinarily, a beginner will first learn *chingmyeong yeombul*, the audible invocation, because it is the foundation of the *yeombul* practice as a whole and aids in one's renunciation of his or her worldly desires.

Yeombul does not entail a complicated procedure, nor does *ganhwaseon*, which calls for a lotus position, but breathing is still important. It is best to do *yeombul* in a comfortable position with a straight back and a long inhalation followed by a slow exhalation. It is especially necessary to concentrate wholeheartedly on the Buddha's name and call it out while attempting to remove the distracting thoughts that might enter one's mind at every moment. It is normally done in a loud voice. The expression "Namu Amit'abul" can be easily heard at temples all around Korea, as well as those in Japan and China. This is the invocation of the Buddha Amitabha.

In some instances, *yeombul* is done at a specific interval, such as every 3, 7 or 21 days. It can also be done at a particular time during a 24-hour period for 30 minutes or an hour. Sometimes, one can strive to repeat the invocation for a set number of times—108; 1,000; or 10,000—in accompaniment to prostration. There is even a form of *yeombul* that continues throughout one's day in a soft voice without interruption of any kind.

Yeombul calls on the practitioner to never rest while reciting the name of the Buddha, to hear the sound of that recitation through one's own ears, and to have faith in the fact that one is indeed the Buddha.

The Temple of Haeinsa in Gyeongsangnam-do is home to the *Tripitaka Koreana*, the most complete collection of Buddhist texts, engraved on 80,000 woodblocks between 1237 and 1248.

Gangyeong and Dokgyeong: Reading the Wisdom of the Buddha

In Korean Buddhism, scriptures are not just books. Scriptures contain the words of the Buddha and record the wisdom that leads to awakening. They are the very place where the Buddha's breath can be felt, and they amount more than just characters. This is why reading the scriptures, both silently and aloud, has remained an important form of practice that imbues one's body and mind with the Buddha's teachings.

Simply put, *gangyeong* and *dokgyeong* are acts of reading scriptures that record the Buddha's message; the former is intended to be read without speaking, while the latter is meant to be read aloud. In the beginning, this was not seen as a practice. It was only later that reading the scriptures was considered to be a form of practice because the scriptures are seen as the body or wisdom of the Buddha. In other words, scriptures are treated very much like pagodas and Buddha statues. Reading them is a practice based on the belief that when you read the scriptures and praise the words of the Buddha you will be reborn in a place without suffering.

But to reach awakening and successfully calm the mind through *gangyeong* and *dokgyeong*, one must have the right attitude toward the scriptures. If you think of them as merely a way to accumulate wisdom, it tends to lead to the accumulation of stubbornness and prejudice about the contents of the scriptures, as well as a tendency to try and distinguish your interpretation from those of others, ultimately resulting in disputes. On the contrary, if you have the belief that the Buddha is preaching the dharma to those who read the scriptures, it will be a great practice that will allow one to understand the truth contained in the scriptures.

Sagyeong: Copying the Words of the Buddha to Ingrain Them in Your Heart

In February 2001, a scripture copied in the blood of an old monk practicing at Geonbongsa Temple was found. He had cut off the tip of his finger so he could use the blood to write the 130 characters from one section of the Avatamsaka Sutra, an important Mahayana text. It caused a huge shock at the time, but the monk's determination to guard and execute the words of the Buddha as though they were his own life was embedded in this practice of "blood-copying."

Lotus Sutra (*Myobeop Yeonhwagyeong*) in silver on oak paper, Goryeo Dynasty, National Treasure No. 185, National Museum of Korea

Copying the scriptures—*sagyeong*—involves duplicating the words of the Buddha, and it has been practiced for a long time in Korean Buddhism. The origin of the practice goes back to the time just after the Buddha's physical form passed away and disciples used a type of wood veneer to record his words in Sanskrit. In Korea, copying was emphasized as a way of widely circulating the Buddha's teaching, and it was most actively done in the Silla and Goryeo Dynasties. Later, copying became established as a form of practice that would discipline a chaotic mind and allow one to immerse oneself in the Buddha's words, rather than as means to circulate the scriptures themselves.

Depending on the material used to copy the scriptures, the practice is divided into different types. One can use ink, gold, silver, or blood.

Sagyeong requires a special mindset, much as *gangyeong* and *dokgyeong* do. It has the purpose of inscribing the Buddha's wisdom in one's mind while copying each character of the text. If you do not concentrate on the words of the Buddha, the Chinese characters can be out of shape or simply incorrect—concentration on the task at hand is crucial.

In the past, it was once popular to practice a form of *sagyeong* that called for either one or three prostrations after writing one character, but this was later discovered to be a Japanese practice, not Korean. This type of *sagyeong* can interfere with one's concentration on the words of the Buddha, so prostrating in between copying is discouraged.

Jeol: Surrendering One's Ego

Jeol is traditionally a form of courtesy that shows respect for others, and its significance is no different in Korean Buddhism. The bow is not to be done mindlessly, but as a practice in search of the Buddha within as one lowers oneself.

Jeol is the most strenuous form of practice at a temple. Foreigners, too, will often encounter *jeol* during a temple stay program, where it is not uncommon to perform 108 prostrations. For the most part, however, the prostrations are done in conjunction with threading 108 wooden beads—one for each prostration.

As with any practice, the mental state of the performer is important. The meaning of *jeol* is that one humbles oneself by bringing one's forehead, elbows, palms, knees, and feet—five parts of the body—into contact with the floor. It is an apology to those who might have been hurt by one's errors in the past, possible only if one lets go of the idea that one is always right; *jeol* is a physical practice that tames such egocentric ideas. Whether you perform the act of submission 108 times or 3,000 times, when you do countless *jeols*, you will naturally find yourself humbled.

Jeol can have the effect of making the mind and body healthy when repetitive action and breathing take place in harmony. *Jeol* begins with *hapjang*—bringing the two palms together before the chest. *Hapjang* allows the body to center itself and strengthen the heart, putting the mind and body at ease. At this point in the exercise, you should not put too much pressure on the palms or tense your muscles. After *hapjang*, slowly bend your toes and kneel down. While doing this movement, breathe in deeply. Put your hands on the floor and place your forehead down as well, placing your left foot over your right, and reverse your palms, raising them heavenward. Now slowly breathe out.

Maintaining this sequence of movements in your performance of *jeol* can also contribute to improving one's health. A Korean TV network SBS aired a documentary titled *The Miracle of 2/3 Square Meters* (2010) that introduced people who had recovered their health by practicing *jeol*. In addition, the Korean public broadcaster KBS did a special New Year's episode of the TV program *The Secrets of Life, Aging, Disease, and Death* in 2008 called "Awaken Your Brain," which highlighted a nine-year practitioner of *jeol*, the custom of 3,000 prostrations, and revealed the mystery of *jeol* as a positive force for increasing concentration.

Vipassana: Examining the Mind

When the Buddha took his last breath, his disciples used the Pali language to recite and record his words. The books written in Pali are called the early Buddhist scriptures. *Vipassana* is a practice systematized on the basis of this set of scriptures, limited to Myanmar, Thailand, and Sri Lanka before becoming more widely known even in Korean Buddhism.

Vipassana has gained special attention because of its history and privileged status as a form of practice based on the earliest recorded scriptures. It was introduced to Korea around 1988. Monk Geohae was instrumental in its early distribution, becoming the first person in the country to practice it and introduce it to a wider public.

All practices prioritize breathing as an important part of the exercise, emphasizing the fact that life depends on each and every breath; every life-form will die if it does not get the oxygen it needs. It is the same in *vipassana*, also known as insight meditation. *Vipassana* is a compound of two Pali words: *vi*, which means "to separate," and *passana*, which means "to observe" or "to stare." In other words, the practice revolves around being conscious of everything, including extraneous thoughts, external sensations, sounds, lights, and many other things. Through breathing in and out and observing the process carefully, insight meditation gathers the mind at the tip of one's nose. When concentrating on one's breathing as one inhales and exhales out of the nose, the mind may travel to the pain in one's legs or other unnecessary thoughts; in these cases, a person must consciously breathe more deeply and return his or her mind back to the tip of their nose. When the mind remains in this place and one continues to be aware of one's breathing, a person's preoccupation with individual breaths disappears, the power of concentration expands, and the mind is made more peaceful.

PRACTICES AVAILABLE DURING TEMPLE STAYS

Temples with programs tailored for foreigners can offer opportunities ranging from simple cultural experiences to formal monastic rituals. It may not be possible to immerse oneself in the intensive practices of Buddhism, but short escapes into the temple lifestyle are often possible.

If you want to heal your exhausted mind or recover your sense of self, seek out Beopjusa Temple in Boeun, Chungcheongbuk-do. Beopjusa runs the "Anger Camp," which takes place in a forest and involves activities that stimulate the five senses—a meditation program with a healing component. Since you meditate under the guidance of medical professionals and psychiatric specialists, you can obtain accurate information about depression and learn to heal yourself through counseling. It is strongly recommended if you are suffering from the "cold of the mind" that is depression.

If you want a short practice experience in the city, Myogaksa Temple is ideal. Among all the Korean temple stay programs, Mogaksa offers the most concentrated, foreigner-friendly learning experience for those who are unable to make an overnight commitment at a temple. The temple has a highly trained staff who speak foreign languages. It offers a four-hour temple life program comprising an orientation session, an introduction to *jeol*, an

explanation of the meaning of 108 prostrations, and a staff-guided demonstration of the practice, including making of the prayer beads. The program has become more widely known thanks to foreigners who have publicized it on social networking sites and blogs.

The Yeondeung International Seon Center, located near one of the oldest temples in Korea, Jeondeungsa Temple, is situated on Ganghwado Island, near Incheon. While *chamseon* and walking meditation are both very accessible here, the center also offers an opportunity for more intensive practice. Though not belonging to the network of temples that specifically cater to foreigners, the center serves as an international institution specializing in the practice of *chamseon* and thus its staff have no communication problems. The center was started by monk Wonmyeong, a disciple of Venerable Master Seongcheol, who was once called the Tiger of Mt. Gayasan for his charismatic leadership at seasonal monastic retreats. It was established with the awareness that foreigners do not have access to many spaces for deep engagement with

chamseon, and its temple stay offerings are designed to uphold that spirit of accessibility.

In addition to the focus on traditional meditation practices, there are other sites that focus on more niche traditions, such as martial arts or tea ceremonies. The aforementioned Golgulsa Temple in Gyeongju, for example, regularly offers a temple stay program that uses the martial art of *sunmudo* to teach foreigners how to discipline both the body and the mind. Jabiseonsa Temple in Seongju, by contrast, will soon hire foreign language interpreters to operate a tea meditation program. Tea was chosen as this temple's focus because of its ability to fill the mind with compassion, and the program is intended to help participants observe each and every change in their minds that derive from to the act of drinking tea.

Besides this, there are programs using *vipassana*, a technique from Southeast Asia that is practiced in such countries as Thailand, Myanmar, and Sri Lanka. Bonginsa Temple does not specialize in programs for foreigners, but is still worth considering for the

opportunity to experience *vipassana* in Korea. As previously discussed, *vipassana*, also known as insight meditation, cultivates the ability to observe the mind. The purpose of the practice is to calm one's thoughts, focusing one's attention on simply breathing in and out. At Bonginsa, the program is led by Venerable Master U Suvanna, who was recognized as an international leader for meditation by the Mahasi Meditation Center in Myanmar.

PRACTICES THAT CAN BE DONE IN DAILY LIFE

At first glance, Buddhist practice may seem hard, so we would like to introduce some practices that might be a bit more accessible for newcomers.

A good place to begin is *jabisugwan*. To practice this form of meditation, first imagine a compassionate hand that cares for your mind with love and empathy. Using your imagination, create a hand that can then be filled with compassion—concentrate on it intently. With this hand, pet, stroke, and embrace your back. It is important to keep it as soft as a mother's touch on a baby. Making the hand is essential. Practice using your imaginative hand to hit a wall, and also attempt to change its length to make it long or short. This type of practice is meant to help cultivate concentration; when the imagination of the hand can be maintained for a long time, use the hand to stroke your painful past or memories as a therapeutic practice. The objective of *jabisugwan* is to use this hand that heals you to transmit warm energy to the minds of those surrounding you.

A similar practice is the five-color tea meditation. When drinking tea, you do not need instruments such as cups when you have the power of imagination. First, relax the mind. Then, build a tea room inside your mind and pour tea into an imagined cup. Pour into the cup tea that has one of the five following colors: gold, white, red,

green, or blue. Feel the warmth and volume of the tea liquid as you drink it and imagine it permeating your body. When you take the tea cup away from you mouth, feel the reaction of your body and mind.

The five different colors effect different psychologies: gold (earth), white (water), red (fire), green (wind), and blue (space). With this meditation, it is possible to bring serenity to the mind. Gold tea will melt away strong ego and pride. White tea turns anger and hatred into generosity and humility. Red tea will convert nervousness and greed into selflessness. Green tea will suppress envy and jealousy, bringing about calmness and restoration of energy. Blue tea will dissolve worries about negative past memories. At this time, compassion as created by the five-color tea meditation will be expressed outwardly, and those in front of you will feel a particular warmth depending on what color of tea you have consumed.

Self-love meditation is also manageable on one's own. Self-love meditation is a way to control the rage inside one's mind, and is known to be an effective way to send energy of love to all beings including oneself. Ultimately, it is a way to eliminate the rage inside

ANGEO: A SPECIAL STUDY BEHIND A LOCKED DOOR

Korean Buddhism has a special type of study that requires locking the door, a tradition of practice known as *angeo*. Twice a year, for three months each in summer and winter, monks are required to focus exclusively on practice.

It is a system based on the historical fact that Buddhism was born in India. Originally, *angeo* was a translation of a Sanskrit word for the monsoon season. During the monsoon season, rivers overflow, roads become submerged, and insects crawl out of the earth. If one walks around during this time it is possible to step on and kill plants and insects. The first rule that all Buddhist practitioners must abide by is to abstain from killing, and in the interest of preventing practitioners from engaging in this act, going out was forbidden. This was the beginning of *angeo*.

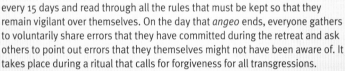

Because of the climate conditions of India, *angeo* always fell during the three months in summer when it rained the most. Therefore, in the beginning, it was only meant to be a summer retreat for monks. But as Buddhism travelled through China and reached Korea, the system of twice-per-year *angeo* was established, once for summer and another for winter.

The start of *angeo* is known as *gyeolje* ("to tie the seal"), and the end is called *haeje* ("to break the seal"). During *angeo*, practitioners come together every 15 days and read through all the rules that must be kept so that they remain vigilant over themselves. On the day that *angeo* ends, everyone gathers to voluntarily share errors that they have committed during the retreat and ask others to point out errors that they themselves might not have been aware of. It takes place during a ritual that calls for forgiveness for all transgressions.

In Korea, the summer *angeo* season is observed from the 15th day of the 4th month to the 15th day of the 7th month, according to the lunar calendar. The winter *angeo* is observed from the 15th day of the 10th month to the 15th day of the 1st month of the following year, again as dictated by the lunar calendar.

During this time one can see the "No entry" sign in different places at Korean Buddhist temples. Even if you participate in temple stay, you must avoid places with such signs, as these are places where monks are devoting themselves to practice during *angeo*.

the mind one step at a time, similar to the Bodhi-mind meditation of Tibetan Buddhism. The Bodhi-mind meditation is also about thinking of everyone near, such as family and friends, and far away, such as those who may have harmed you or caused you to be angry, all with the purpose of generating a mind (a Bodhi mind) that will wish them awakening. It is based on the teaching of the Buddha that all beings in this world are connected. People around are believed to have been or have the destiny of becoming your parents, friends, or children in your previous or future life.

If *ganhwaseon* is too difficult, it is not a bad idea to start out with an easier practice: *susikgwan*. Assume the lotus position, straighten your back, and count numbers in your mind. While breathing through the nose, count from 1 to 10, counting simultaneously with exhalation. When you focus exclusively on the numbers, all extraneous thoughts, anxiety, and depression will disappear, leaving only numbers. It is a way to suppress bad thoughts. When you get used to *susikgwan* and are able to remain focused on the numbers, it is time to advance to *ganhwaseon*.